Add-On Selling

How to Squeeze Every Last Ounce of Sales Potential From Your Calls

Jim Domanski

Business Inc.
By Phone

13254 Stevens St., Omaha, NE 68137 402-895-9399 Fax: 402-896-3353
www.businessbyphone.com

Add-On Selling
How to Squeeze Every Last Ounce of Sales Potential
From Your Calls
By Jim Domanski

Published By:
Business By Phone Inc.
13254 Stevens St.
Omaha, NE 68137.
(402)895-9399
Fax:(402)896-3353
E-mail arts@businessbyphone.com
http://www.businessbyphone.com

Author: Jim Domanski
Jim Domanski
613 591 1998
jdomanski@igs.net
http://www.teleconceptsconsulting.com

Cover design by George Foster, Foster & Foster, Fairfield, IA

ISBN 978-1-881081-11-1

Table of Contents

Chapter 1

Add-On Selling–
An Overview

If you are leafing through this book right now, you are either
a prospective buyer or you are a customer who has already
bought it. Either way, if you read nothing else, read this
chapter. It will orient you on what the book is all about
and what it can do for you.

Here's what you are going to find in this chapter. First of
all, we'll look at what I mean by "add-on selling." Once
you understand precisely what add-on selling is, we can
then move on to examine the thirteen strategic opportunities
that add-on selling presents. If you are real anxious, here
are the thirteen applications. There is more detail on each within
the next couple of pages.

1: Up-Selling
2: Cross-selling
3: Converting Inquires
4: Converting Cancellations
5: Selling on Complaint Calls
6: Gathering Market Intelligence
7: Getting a Referral
8: Generating and Qualifying a Lead
9: Selling on a Collections Call
10: Selling on the Service Call
11: Selling on the Internet
12: Down-Selling
13: The Outbound Call

This part of the book is important. It will give you a concise view of the applications that can make a difference in the way you sell and service your clients.

We'll close the chapter with "Who should read this book?" Inevitably, when I mention Add-on Selling there are those who raise their hands and say, "It doesn't apply to me or my job."

Bull.

Chances are it does. If you interface with any of your customers or prospects, then add-on selling can apply.

What is Add-On Selling?

Let me cut to the chase and explain what add-on selling is.

> The process of leveraging a customer or prospect contact by generating *additional* revenues, or by generating a *marketing opportunity*.

Another way of putting it is that add-on selling is a way to maximize every dialogue you have with a client or a prospect. It is a way to grab and squeeze every single ounce of opportunity from an inbound or outbound call. It is a simple, easy to use, no fuss and no muss way to increase sales or to create a sales opportunity.

Marketing Opportunity?

But what do I mean by a "marketing opportunity?" A marketing opportunity is anything of value that might assist in the sales process. For instance, a marketing opportunity would be getting *a referral* after an order has been taken because a referral can change to a lead and a lead to a sale. Or, it might be qualifying a lead after an inquiry, which can be passed on to a sales team who can possibly convert it. Later on you will see that it can also refer to gathering market, product, or competitive intelligence by "adding on" a few questions, and the information obtained can be used to improve products, develop new markets, etc. Whatever the application, it will help you and your company.

The Sad Reality in Sales and Marketing

The potential to increase sales and marketing opportunities for you and your company is limitless. The reason for this is that so few people employ the concept, which in turn gives you a distinct, competitive advantage.

I want you to think about this for a moment. You or your company have worked long and hard to reach your customers or prospects. You might have used direct mail, fax or e-mail to get your target to pick up the phone and place an order or inquire about a product or service. Or, you may have spent countless hours dialing numbers, encountering hard-nosed secretaries or dealing with voice mail. Either way, you have finally got "The MAN", also known as the decision maker, the person with the bucks, the one who spends. It was a tough haul but here he is, on the line.

A good deal of time and money was spent to get you this far.

But here's the really sad part of it. The vast majority of call centers and sales organizations are content with just that. They are content to only take the call or handle the inquiry. On the outbound side, they are only too content to make the sale or generate the lead. They leave it like this. Mission accomplished.

What makes this rather pathetic is that after all the toil and trouble to get to the target market, we do nothing more to leverage it. Here you are, finally, one-to-one with your target market and you do nothing more with it. In that call you have any number of opportunities to maximize the relationship.

But you are not alone in this scenario. If you are guilty, then so too are your competitors. Again, I say most organizations do not leverage the opportunity. What this really means is that if you can develop your add-on strategy with your customers, you become more successful and more profitable.

Manipulative?

Before we go any further, let's clear up something. When I refer to "add-on selling" I am not talking about sleazy and manipulative selling tips and techniques that are designed to take advantage of a buyer. Some people equate add-on selling with slimy, force-fed offers and clever tricks; unloading junk and raising the revenue of the sale for the sheer greed of it. While I know there are those who would do this, I certainly do not advocate the approach. We'll look at this a little deeper in a later chapter entitled, "The Dark Side". But for now, I am talking about a *consultative, client focused* approach to your customers and prospects. I am talking about methods that *add value* and definitely don't take advantage of the relationship.

Everything in this book, everything, is designed for the long-term benefit of the client, for you, and for your company. Okay?

And as Martha Stewart might say, "That's a good thing."

Let's take a quick look at the add-on strategies.

13 Strategic Opportunities

Lucky 13! There are at least thirteen add-on selling and marketing opportunities or strategies that can help you leverage the call or the relationship, and I have a chapter on each one. Here's a quick overview to let you know what's ahead.

Add-On Strategy 1: Up-Selling

Up-Selling is a term used to define the process of increasing the value of a sale by adding on more quantity of a given product. For example, moving a client from four units to six units. It is also a term used for increasing the value by up-selling the quality of a given product.

Add-On Strategy 2: Cross-Selling

Ever been to McDonald's? (Gee, talk about your rhetorical question.)

Have you ever ordered a hamburger and the server says, "Would you like fries with that today?"

That's a cross-sell. And it works.

Cross-selling is the process of add-on selling by adding a related (or sometimes non-related) item. Usually, but not always, the item will complement the original purchase. Let me tell you a secret. There are two reasons why customers don't buy more products from you:

- they don't know you have it, and,

- you don't ask them if they want it.

Add-On Strategy 3: Converting an Inquiry

Not many people realize that over 60% of inquiries end without some sort of action on behalf of the customer. And about 30% of these inquirers actually intended to buy–and ultimately do so–either with you at a later date or with your competitor. Simply by asking for a sale after you handle the inquiry can garner more revenues. Unfortunately, the average customer service rep doesn't know how to ask for the sale.

Add-On Strategy 4:
Converting a Cancellation

Customer service, order desk, and help desk reps will recognize this one. Customers call in to cancel an order or perhaps a subscription or service...whatever. Dutifully, the service rep takes the information and makes the cancellation. What a travesty! Asking a few questions and learning why the cancellation is occurring might reveal an opportunity to keep the order from being terminated. Sometimes it's a complaint, sometimes it's an inappropriate product. Whatever the reason, the opportunity to suggest an alternative or to solve a problems exists.

Add-On Strategy 5: Selling on a Complaint

You wouldn't think that you could sell to an angry customer, would you? You can. It's been done. Value the angry customer because they often tell you what you are doing wrong. Effectively solve a problem for a customer and they tend to be receptive to any add-on sale you might have simply because you stuck by them and helped them when the problem occurred. Most people want a resolution. Once they get it, they are only too happy to listen further.

Add-On Strategy 6:
Gathering Market Intelligence

This strategy can be used in just about every customer or prospect contact situation. By simply asking a few questions of your caller after the initial order, request, etc. has been taken, you can uncover dozens of opportunities. The one-to-one dialogue with literally hundreds of clients can give you a quick snapshot of competitors, of the customers' needs, and of market conditions. You name it. Machiavelli

said "Information is power." Here's a way to get it
without going to a market research firm and paying
thousands of dollars.

Add-On Strategy 7: Getting a Referral
Field reps and inside reps pay close heed to this
one. If you have done a decent job and if your product or
service has truly helped a client, then asking for a referral
is a darned good idea. The simple truth of the matter is
that most reps don't want to appear intrusive by asking
their clients for referrals. Fine. In the meantime, those
that do are blowing the tops off their sales objectives. Clients
will give you referrals from time to time. The trick is
how to ask effectively. And let me add-one other thing.
What's the absolute worst a customer can say? If you've
done your job effectively, the worst they can say is "no". I
have been teaching and consulting for close to twenty
years. In that time, not one single rep who has asked for a
referral has been slapped, much less shouted at. The consequences are minimal. Ask.

Add-On Strategy 8:
Generating and Qualifying a Lead
Here is an absolutely massive opportunity for those of you
in customer service, inside sales, field sales reps, help
desks, etc. After the call has been handled, ask a few
questions related to a product or service. If those questions
have been well thought out and planned, they can tell
you whether or not you have a lead.

Whether you convert it, or it is done by someone else, the
point is you have created an opportunity. It scares the
heck out of me when I think of how many call centers
by-pass this strategy. It's a crying shame.

Add-on Strategy 9: The Collections Call

I know what you are thinking. "Selling on a collections call? Ya gotta be kidding me?"

Not every call is made to a deadbeat account. Some calls are made to those who can pay but won't. They won't pay because they usually have a gripe, a beef, or a complaint and they are withholding the funds to get some sort of response or to use it as leverage. The trick is to solve the problem. Once you do that, there might be an opportunity to use add-on selling.

Add-On Strategy 10: The Service Call

Service/Repair/Help Desk personnel can make great sales people. There's a simple psychology behind this concept. Service people (I'll use this term to collectively refer to repair personnel, help desk reps, etc.) typically help customers solve problems. They are "saints" and "saviors" for many. Much like customer service reps, service people are not perceived as "sales people". Consequently, their "recommendations" are taken very seriously and are often acted upon. So there is some real potential.

The problem is that service people don't see themselves as sales people. Moreover, they are not trained on selling techniques. As a result, most service people fix the problem and leave it at that when, in fact, the customer is receptive to any sales message they might have that relates to their current situation. Training service people on how to provide a simple, benefit-oriented sales message can result in significant revenues or leads.

Add–On Strategy 11: The Internet

The last time I looked, about fifteen minutes ago, the Internet is still booming in leaps and bounds. It is a whole new form of communications with prospects and customers, and one that invites add-on selling. I am not simply talking about "e-commerce" application, although the opportunity for add-on selling is ripe. I am talking about using add-on selling in 3-mails and e-messaging, such as newsletters and web sites. While this application is a little more passive, it still presents a great way to sell more.

Add-On Strategy 12: Down-Selling
Hold on, Tex! What gives here?
Can you sell more by selling less? You can bet your bottom dollar you can! In some situations, the client relationship in the long term is more important than the money in the short term. What this really means is that sometimes it is wiser to consultant with a client and 'down-sell' on a product or service simply because you know it could create long term resentment. However, the upside of down-selling is that you get repeat customers due to the satisfaction that is generated.

Add-On Strategy 13: The Outbound Call
Not everyone is willing to do this one extra step, particularly if you work in an inbound call center, but the outbound follow-up call can mean a windfall of revenues. It has been shown that 87% of sales reps give up after a single contact with a prospect. Persistence is non-existent. If you really want to leverage a relationship, you'll have to follow-up on the interest or leads that you have generated. Persistence pays.

Remember when we talked about converting cancellations? Sometimes the cancellations are requested by direct mail, e-mail, or fax. Why not pick up the phone and see why? You might salvage a few.

Suppose a client who orders regularly doesn't call this month? Should you wait to see what happens next month, or do you pick up the phone and go for it? This has tons of potential.

Who Should Read This Book?

You've had a good glance at the add-on strategies. It should be clear who could benefit from this book. But let's take a closer look.

Inside Sales Reps

If you are an inside sales rep making outbound calls to prospects or clients, this book is a must. There is not another way to describe it. It will not only identify strategies, it will give you specific tips and techniques on how to conduct "add-on selling". They are practical tips, which are easy to learn, and easy to use. They are proven. Others have used them. No theory here. What this really means to you is a method of achieving your objectives in less time, with less hassle, and with greater success. And if you are on any sort of commission or incentive plan, this gives you some powerful ways to increase your paycheck, just buy the book now. You'll be glad you did.

Field Sales Reps

If you are a field sales rep, I hope you made it this far. While this book is about leveraging an inbound or an outbound call, it is really about leveraging a relationship. Whether that relationship is by phone or face-to-face doesn't really matter. Most of the strategies and techniques described here are easily transferable to a face-to-face selling or service situation. Besides, chances are you use the phone everyday whether it is for setting appointments, following up, or whatever. The tips in here will prove to be priceless. Bottom line? If you are on commission or bonus, then you can't pass this up because it is your opportunity to excel.

Customer Service Reps

If you handle inquiries, process orders, or even take complaints, this book is brimming with ideas on how to leverage those types of calls and increase sales and sales opportunities. Let's be straight and honest here for a moment. Most CSRs resist the concept of "selling". If you are like most CSRs, you might feel that "selling" is simply too assertive and that the customer or prospect won't like it. There's more on this in a moment, but for now you should realize that the average customer or prospect not only wants but needs a more assertive, consultative rep to help him/her attain more value. This book demonstrates how you can give better customer service through add-on selling. It does it with real life examples and no-bull techniques that are appreciated by customers and prospects. If you want to do more for your clients, if you want to move on in your career, take a long hard look at what's inside.

Field Sales Managers

If you are charged with maximizing revenues in your sales territory, then you have to pick this book up. Sorry. No other way to say it. Most sales reps do not know how to leverage a sales opportunity and maximize the revenues. I think you know this somewhere deep inside. This book not only reveals the fact that opportunities exists, it shows you how to implement them. Let me put it in a language that you can probably understand more easily. The book offers ways to help your sales reps, and YOU, achieve and exceed sales revenues.

Inbound Call Center Supervisors and Managers

If you have an inbound call center, you will want to keep this book front and center, particularly if you are looking to shift your call center from a "cost" orientation to a "profit orientation". The tips and techniques offered through the book are so simple and so easy to use that implementing them will be like a walk in the park. Of course, what that really means to you and your company is the opportunity to add more value to the inbound call.

It doesn't matter if your call center handles inquiries or complaints, or acts as a help desk, there are dozens of opportunities to do more for your clients and prospects.

Outbound Call Center Supervisors and Managers

If you're an outbound call center supervisor or manager, chances are you are already in a selling mode. Even if you are collecting overdue accounts, your reps are technically 'selling.' In either case, this book is a veritable road map on how to increase the value of a sale.

Business-to-business, decision maker contact rates are hovering at 30-40%. This means that for every call your reps make, they only reach three to four decision makers. I don't know about you, but to me that's not staggering. What it means to most call center managers is that for the call center to be as effective and profitable as it can be, the rep must use that contact wisely. Getting your outbound rep to add-on sell spells profitability. It spells effectiveness. It spells customer satisfaction.

This book tells you how to do it. It's like a secret recipe for success. Keep it under lock and key because others will want to snatch it away from you.

Service Advisors, Technicians, and Repair

If you work with customers after the sale, you might want to leaf through a few chapters. Customers don't label you as a "sales person". Your job, in their eyes, is to help or assist in some fashion. And because they don't have a sales perception about you, they are open to your suggestions, ideas, and recommendations. It's true. By the way, I am not talking about manipulating your position simply to sell. I am talking about recognizing an opportunity where the customer wins and you win by selling or promoting an idea or service. In doing so, you bring more value to the client. Clients like value. Clients stick with vendors and service providers who give value. Clients give referrals to those they like. They buy more. Get the message?

Summary

Add-on selling is a powerful way to increase sales and marketing opportunities. It can work in a wide variety of situations with a wide variety of personnel. It is something you must do. Read on!

Chapter 2

The Nine Good Reasons (Benefits) Why You Should Implement Add-On Selling

Do you need a little bit of convincing about the benefits of add-on selling? Maybe you need to sell the concept to someone. Maybe you're not sure of yourself. If either of these are the case, this chapter is for you. It looks at the nine reasons why add-on selling makes good financial sense and customer sense.

Don't Assume

One of the biggest mistakes made by sales reps is that they assume their customers and prospects readily understand the benefits of what they are offering. How do you spell disaster?

Being well aware of that particular mistake, let me list the benefits of add-on selling for you and/or your call centre or sales force. I think you can intuitively grasp the obvious, but let's take a closer look.

1. Add-on selling increases revenue.

Okay, we've hammered this one home earlier but it is worth a second look. In these competitive days, it is teeth-gnashingly tough to get a customer or prospect to pick up the phone and call. It is even tougher for you to pick up the phone and reach your clients and prospects. My point is, when you have finally made a sale or taken the order, leverage the moment. Take the opportunity to increase the volume, cross-sell, or whatever is appropriate.

Let me ask you a question. What would happen if 10% of the customers you sold to increased their order size by 10-20%? How would that affect your objectives or your commission? Now, what happens if the total number of those who bought more rose to 15-20%? How about 25%?

Do the math. Work it out yourself. Assuming you have a decent product or service, having 20% of your client base accept an add-on sell is not atypical. In some cases, it has been as much as 40%. Forty percent! Can you imagine? Simply because they asked.

Sales are about revenues. Add-on selling is about *increasing* revenues.

2. Add-on selling reduces costs.
The second benefit is related to the first. Finding a customer and getting a sale is an expensive proposition. Here's a little quiz:

What is your cost of generating an inquiry?

How many inquiries or leads before you get a sale?

What is your total cost of generating a sale?

How much is an average sale for you?

I'll bet you dollars to donuts that you're not sure of any of these costs. If you take the time to learn, you will recognize that the cost of a sale is often staggering. Particularly where field sales reps are concerned, all sorts of surveys covering a variety of industries will peg the cost of a visit, much less a sale at $200.00, at $400.00, some over $1000.00. Of course, a call center cost-per-call and cost-per-sale will be somewhat less. Nonetheless, it is all relative. To make a sale, it costs money.

It ain't cheap, son.

So what would happen if you sold more product on the call?

The cost of the sale goes down. Do that 25% of the time and the costs go down significantly. Do that with **all** of your sales reps and the cost of running your call center goes down. That means you're more profitable. It might mean a better commission or a fatter bonus. Call me a mad cap crazy, but I have always found that owners, presidents, and accountants like profit.

3. It creates a profit center vs. call center.
Customer service managers or supervisors take heed: If you have a customer service call center, chances are you are perceived as a "cost center". Let me translate that more succinctly: you are seen as a "necessary evil". That's the truth.

But what would happen if you could transform your call center into a profit center?

Suddenly you are seen in a new light. Executives get happier. They give you bigger budgets. You have some control over your destiny. Not bad for a little add-on selling.

4. Add-on selling increases customer share.
"Customer share" is one of those sexy marketing phrases and it refers to how much of the customer's business a company gets. A good example is a business that buys office supplies. The customer calls Company A and buys

paper and presentation products. She calls Company B for office furniture and Company C for coffee, bathroom, and cleaning supplies. Most office supply companies sell all these products but it is typical in the industry that the customer buys separately.

Why?

Because no one has told them or no one has asked them. By the way, get used to this phrase as I am going to be stating if fairly often.

Add-on selling means acquiring all the business - customer share.

5. Add-on selling increases the perception of value.
When done effectively, add-on selling is of value to the client. By advising the client how they might save money is value. By educating the client of special offers or of other products that may help them creates value. The rep is seen as "consultative" and helpful, not pushy and aggressive.

6. Add-on selling reduces attrition.
Every company has attrition. Every company loses a percentage of clients for a variety of reasons. But the number one reason customers leave is due to neglect. A full 68% of clients leave not because of price, not because of a product, not because of a complaint, but because of neglect.

Neglect, of course, has many meanings. I would hazard a guess that neglect also refers to simply giving the client plain, vanilla, mediocre service. Heck, they can get that anywhere. The company that educates its client base, that solicits and responds to their comments, that brings value from time to time, is the company who reduces attrition

...which increases profits...which grows market share...
and so on. Catch my drift?

7. Add-on selling generates opportunities.

We've talked about this already, but let's revisit it for a
moment. An inbound call center takes hundreds of calls
per day. This means hundreds of opportunities to
dialogue with the caller. Use that opportunity to ask
questions and learn. Find out what they think of your
products or your competitors' products. Speak to the people
who matter - your clients. If you have a field sales force,
work with them and determine how you might qualify the
caller for other products or services. The opportunities
are endless if you take the time to think it out.

8. If you don't do it, someone else will.

I am appealing to the fear motivator here. If you don't
employ the strategy of add-on selling, your competitor
will. It's too compelling not to. If you look back a page or
two and examine the benefits of increasing customer
share, reducing attrition, and perception of value added,
you will see some solid reasons why a more 'proactive'
approach to the market makes sense. You'll also see that
the company or person who employs them first has a huge
advantage. Think about it.

9. Add-on selling works and it is easy to implement.

Hey, I am the first to admit that add-on selling is not
rocket science - quite the opposite. It's easy to implement.
It requires a little thought, some planning, and some
Training, but that's about it. This book will help you
handle that side of the equation. Lastly, add-on selling works.
You've seen it at McDonalds. Not everyone says yes but
many do. And McDonalds is more profitable for it.

Summary

I probably could have articulated a number of other Benefits, but I think this covers the most critical. However, despite the compelling nature of these benefits, there is still resistance to add-on selling. We'll look at that in the next chapter.

Chapter 3

Add-On Selling Resistance, And What To Do About It

The benefits of add-on selling are overwhelming, yet the resistance to the concept continually staggers me. In this chapter, we'll take a look at the four major reasons why companies and sales and customer service reps tend to avoid implementing an add-on selling program.

Reason 1: "Our Customers Won't Like It."

This is one of the most popular excuses for not implementing add-on selling programs, particularly with inbound call centers.

The word "excuses" is used deliberately because the cold, hard truth is that most *customers do not mind an add-on.* Done properly, your customers like it. Many of them love it. Research shows that a staggering 87% of those clients surveyed said they *wanted* to know of any special offers, and were quite receptive to providing information if they felt it might be beneficial. Some went so far as to say that they would be annoyed or upset if they *were not* advised of an offer that might benefit them. So, think about what you're really giving your customers.

What customers and prospects do mind and don't like can be boiled down to three distinct areas:

A. They don't like aggressive add-on selling.

It is not the add-on sell itself that customers don't like but rather the *manner* in which it is delivered. The number one complaint with customers is reps that just won't quit. They are like those irritating little terrier dogs that relentlessly yip and yap and nip at your cuff. As you will see, the add-on is a casual mention of a special offer or suggestion. If the customer declines, no problem. Accept it and get over it.

Nothing, absolutely nothing, annoys customers more than a rep who continues to jam information down the listener's throat, or the rep that tries to hard-sell an unrelated item. This type of behavior not only sullies the add-on sell, it weakens the entire contact. It could result in a loss of a sale or the loss of a customer for life.

You don't like aggressive reps. I don't like them. Your customers don't like them either.

B. They don't like unprofessional attempts to pitch products.

A pathetic, halfhearted attempt at an add-on is nearly as annoying as the aggressive attempt. Customers recognize when reps are simply going through the motions by making a lackluster offer.

Again, the issue here is not the add-on itself but the manner in which it is delivered. A lazy, mumbled suggestion does not inspire a customer to take action - just the opposite. Similarly, the rep that delivers the offer in staccato fashion simply to 'get it over with' turns customers off. Here's an add-on sale I recently experienced:

"I doubt if you would be interested, but we do have
a special of the month that I could tell you about."
The rep was right. Because it was delivered in such
a negative manner, I wasn't interested.

Unprofessional. Bored. Tired. Forced. Canned.

The point is simply this: if you are not going to do
it right, don't bother doing it at all. You'll create
problems rather than opportunities.

C. They don't like unrelated items.

This reason has to be qualified to some extent.
Customers don't like an add-on if they don't
understand the nature of the add-on. Here's a real
life example. Suppose you were buying a printer
for your computer at an electronics shop and the
rep says, "Oh, by the way, we have space heaters on
sale."

How would you feel? What would you think?

Printers and space heaters? Where the heck is the
relationship? They are so totally unrelated that
the offer makes no sense. It's bewildering and
foolish.

With that said, let me offer an exception. There
are times when it is okay to mention an unrelated
item. It depends on what the item is, the cost, and
how it is introduced to the client. This will be
discussed in the cross-selling chapter. But for now,
just recognize that certain unrelated items will sell.

Strategies to Manage Customer Resistance

If you know what customers dislike about add-on selling, then it is relatively simple to build a strategy to manage it.

Provide Knowledge and Skills Training

Gee, that's a no-brainer. But it is critical and it is something that is so often ignored by companies who implement some sort of add-on selling program. I suspect the reason why training of any sort is not provided is because add-on selling looks so easy - just add a line or two to a script and that's it.

Well, yes, it is that easy in some cases, but there's a little more to it than that. For example, listening skills are vital. Has the client exhibited buying or non-buying signals? What do the reps do when confronted with an objection? What if the rep is asked to describe the add-on or the rationale behind it? These nit-picky little things need to be addressed and they spell the difference between "professional" and "non professional".

Provide Monitoring and Coaching

Spend time on this strategy if you want to truly benefit from an add-on selling.

If there is one thing that is lacking in the vast majority of inbound and outbound call centers, as well as in field sales rep development, it is active and ongoing coaching. It's as though organizations say, "We've provided the training, that's it. Now go to it." That's like planting flowers and not watering them.

The training will not amount to much without some sort of reinforcement. That reinforcement comes from monitoring (i.e., observing/listening to the rep during an add-on) and in the form of coaching after the add-on has been conducted. Coaching takes what the rep has learned and provides feedback and support during the actual sales or customer service transaction. You see, what you are doing when you introduce add-on selling is changing the learned behavior of your reps. You are getting them to break habits. It takes twenty-one days to break a habit and about ninety days to change a behavior.

Monitoring and coaching are your insurance policies against unprofessional and assertive add-on selling which annoys the client.

If you are honestly serious about add-on selling, commit to coaching. Don't skimp on it. And if you can't monitor and coach, don't even bother implementing the program. You'll waste time and money. More importantly, it will annoy your customers. Worse, you may lose them.

Select your products and your approach wisely.
One of the biggest sins in add-on selling is using the opportunity to dump junk. What I mean by this is getting rid of products that are poor in quality or have no real value to a customer. This is probably why these items weren't selling in the first place.

While you might get rid of the product, the long-term effect can be disastrous. The customer receives the add-on and sooner or later discovers the product is lousy, lacks value, or performs poorly. The customer may react by sending it back, which is a hassle in itself, but more often than not, they simply shut up and take their business elsewhere. They feel ripped off, and inevitably they tell a bunch of their friend and colleagues. You know what I'm talking about. The real point is, the add-on selling strategy is doomed for failure at some point.

In a non-selling situation, for example, gathering market intelligence, be very, very selective in the types of questions you ask. You need to keep the questions to a minimum and make sure the questions you do ask are exactly what you want. Don't squander the minute or two that the client gives you.

Reason 2: The Reps Don't Like It
Customer Service Applications
There is some merit to this point. Some reps don't like the concept of an add-on sell regardless of whether it is a selling or a marketing application.

This is understandable.

The reps that resist add-on selling typically come from customer service environments. They have been hired to *react* to a customer inquiry, order, complaint, whatever. The best way I can describe the reaction comes from the old Star Trek television series. At some point in the show, Dr. McCoy, the ship's passionate and trusty physician, is asked by Captain Kirk to do something which he has not been hired or trained to do. McCoy will typically reply, "I'm a doctor Jim, not a magician." Well, in the customer service world, the McCoy reply might be, *"I'm a customer service rep, Jim, not a sales rep."*

By their very nature, customer service reps are passive. They were hired, and rightly so, to react to a customer call and provide whatever service is necessary. The customer dictates the terms. The rep responds.

Add-on selling changes the complexion of things. The rep must move from reactive to proactive and from passive to assertive. These traits go against the grain of what they are used to. So, naturally, they dislike it. It's more work on the one hand, but more significantly, it might mean annoying the customer and having to deal with "rejection".

No one really likes rejection, but this is particularly true
in customer service scenarios.

Sales Applications

Interestingly, there are quite a number of inside and
outside sales reps who "dislike" add-on selling. There are
a couple of reasons for this. First, while they are more
assertive in nature, they tend to believe that the add-on will
jeopardize the sale because the rep is coming on too strong.
The rationale is similar to those of the customer service reps.

Secondly, there are those reps who feel they have done
enough. The sale has been made - on to the next one. Why
spend more time on piddly little add-ons when there are
bigger fish to fry? It is kind of sad, but it is true.

Strategies for Dealing With Rep Resistance

Let's face it, if you don't win the hearts and minds of our
Reps, the add-on isn't going to work. And, if you are a sales
rep or a customer service rep and if you have doubt about the
entire process, I can guarantee you that you won't succeed
nearly as well as you would if you believe in what you are
doing.

The following are some strategies to deal with rep reluctance.

Communicate

Duh! There's a thought!

Kidding aside, the whole process starts with education.
You must fully understand that add-on selling conducted
in a professional manner brings greater value to the customer
In effect, you are giving better service. Here's why.

First of all, clients don't buy more or do more for you because they don't know any better. By that I mean they don't buy more from you because you have not told them; you haven't educated them. You deal with your products every day, they don't. You might think they should know your entire product line, but guess what? They don't. Educating them makes them aware of what you have and what you can provide. This can possibly save them money, or time or effort or any number of benefits.

Secondly, as we already know, 87% of customers surveyed said they *wanted to know about an add-on*. Think about that one for a moment. If you don't tell the customer about an add-on, you are actually giving them poorer service. In fact, some will complain that they weren't told of a special, an offer, or a discount. So, look at it this way, the customer is telling you that this is want they want in terms of service.

Thirdly, we know what the average customer doesn't want. They don't want unprofessional and/or overly assertive attempts. That's easy enough to manage.

One last point: if the add-on sell is professionally presented in a friendly, if not consultative manner, what is the absolute worst a customer can say? 'No'. That's it. Nothing more.

So, let's recap. Add-on selling is better customer service.

Finally, on the topic of communicating, communicate the results of the efforts back to your service reps. Nothing will change a behavior quicker than good results. If you can demonstrate that customer satisfaction has improved since the add-on program was introduced, herald it. Blow trumpets. Have a party. Dance in the streets.

Selection of Application and Introduction
Add-on selling should be seen as a long-term strategy, not a one-time shot. Take your time and do it right. Be wise

on the selection of your add-on application. For instance, if you want to sell on an inquiry, start with smaller ticket items; items that are easy to mention and do not require a good deal of thought by the caller. This helps reduce the rejection rate in the early stages of the program. Reduce discouragement.

In the above example you might even want to start with having the reps add two or three market intelligence questions. Find out what your customer is thinking about. Don't worry so much about the nature of the questions, but rather focus on getting the reps to take the initiative after a call has been handled. Move them gradually from reactive to proactive.

Provide Training
Double duh! The only way to overcome the real and perceived fears of the customer service reps is to provide training. Training does not necessarily mean three weeks of classroom workshops. The amount and type of training will vary depending on the nature of your add-on selling application.

(Hey, here's an idea. Why not buy them a copy of this book and have your reps do some "homework". Despite the blatant and unabashed pitch, it is a very effective way to begin the training process without having to spend as much time in the classroom. This saves you time and effort. I like that idea!)

Whatever you do, make sure your training includes role-play sessions. Everyone is usually uptight about practicing in front of peers. So what! They'll get used to it in a short while, especially if it is a fun atmosphere. Bottom line? They'll perform better and with greater confidence when they're on the phones. Just do it.

Remember one important thing: the average customer service rep will resist most add-on applications. They'll resist passively or actively, but generally they'll resist. So

what this really says is that you are better to err on the
side of over-training than under-training.

Provide Job Aids

There is a chapter on job aids, but for now let's just say a
job aid is a tool to help in the add-on selling process. It
might be a simple paper script listing the product or
questions that a rep might ask. It acts as a prompt, a road
map, or a guide to implementing the add-on.

Some companies use "pop up" menus on their computer
screens. For example, a caller might order a Works software package. When the order is entered, a pop-up menu
presents itself on the screen and reminds the rep that
Norton Utilities is on sale. Very effective if you can
implement it.

Other job aids include product descriptions to help describe a product or service. Another very important tool is
an "objections" chart for products or services where a
client might require additional information.

Provide Coaching

As discussed above, coaching will make or break your add-
on program. Customer service reps are being asked to do
something that is generally foreign to them. Support,
feedback, recognition, and correction, particularly in the
early stages of the add-on program, are vital.

I don't want to beat this horse to death... well, maybe I
do. Coaching is the key. Coaching takes time and effort. If
you can't do this, don't bother implementing the program -
you'll just create more problems.

Provide a Reward

This strategy can be a little tricky, if only due to the fact that
it requires some thought. You are asking customer service
reps to do more than what they had originally been hired to do.
If the add-on application involves selling, and you can track

it, you might want to consider a bonus, a commission, or a simple raise in salary.

There are other things you can do that doesn't involve money. Buy a copy of Dave Worman's book, *Motivating Without Money,* published by the same publishers of this book, Business By Phone (800-326-7721 or, 402-895-9399, or www.BusinessByPhone.com). It's worth every dime.

Recognize success and achievement. Doing this makes the entire program rewarding, not only for the rep, but also for the call center and the company.

Reason 3: Add-on Selling Doesn't "Fit" In Our Company

Here's another reason why companies or departments decide not to implement a program, and on the surface, it makes a good deal of sense. It stems from the word "selling". Some companies or individuals do not see a "pure" *sales application* based on the calls they make or take.

E.C.H.O.

Somewhere I read or heard the term "E.C.H.O." used in a call center environment. It stands for "every call has opportunity". It's a great acronym and it can be used as a 'mantra' in any and every call center.

Obviously, some calls don't lend themselves to the "sale" of products or services. Fine. But as we have already shown, there are numerous other applications designed to *leverage* the contact with the client. For instance, gathering competitive intelligence, learning how a customer uses a product, building a buyer profile, or generating a lead or a referral are just a few of the applications. Sales, marketing, and manufacturing would love your help. Executives are pretty keen on customer feedback as well.

Strategy to Consider

Think, Ask and Plan
If you are one of those who feels selling just doesn't fit, go back and read Chapter 1. It will show you that "add-on selling" has multiple meanings. Start there.

Using that information, look at your call center or your department or organization and ask yourself openly, "How could I leverage the caller contact?" Scratch the surface and you'll find plenty of opportunity.

One thing you might do is ask other departments. Sales departments are usually only too willing to get involved. Perhaps a lead generation program can be developed.

Marketing people can have a field day with add-on selling applications. Asking your callers what they think, want, or desire is an inexpensive form of market "research". Heck, what a concept - asking the customers what they really want! Go figure.

Summary
Let's go back to E.C.H.O. Every Call Has Opportunity. There is no real reason not to implement some sort of add-on selling application other than lack of desire. So, take a look at how you are taking or making calls. Determine the opportunity. Analyze why you haven't implemented the strategy before and then develop a plan.

Chapter 4

The Four-Step System To Add-On Selling

Read this chapter and get to know it well. In it, you will find the fundamental structure that virtually every add-on selling situation will take. Well, there are one or two situations where it doesn't quite apply, but we'll point those out. I call it a "system" and I describe it below. You will see the system more or less repeated through the add-on selling chapters.

System Selling

Remember system selling? I talked about it in the introduction, but if you're like me, you skip the introduction and jump into the meat and potatoes of a book, so let me give you an explanation.

I am a big believer in "system selling". That's a term I have coined that refers to the process of breaking down certain selling situations into key parts. Mastering each part in order creates a system. I coach kids' football and hockey. To teach young children how to do a three-point stance in football seems easy enough, but if they have never played and they are nine or ten years old, you better have a system to impart the knowledge. Once the kids learn it, they operate on auto-pilot. They do it automatically That's the goal of the four-step system to add-on selling.

Let's take a more "mature" sports analogy. If you are a golfer, or a tennis player, you know that your swing or stroke can be broken into manageable parts. Master each part one by one and the system is complete.

Going back to my coaching experience, I have seen kids develop in hockey from the time they were five years old (when my son started) until now at age fourteen. I have seen very talented hockey players who do not achieve their potential simply because they have not had a system of play. Equally, I have seen players who were not exceptionally talented but performed well because they play by a disciplined system of hockey.

I am absolutely convinced that if you have a system for add-on selling, and you *manage* the system, you can be successful in sales, and in this case, add-on selling, even if you lack "natural" sales talent. If you are talented or a naturally gifted salesperson, then the system will make you even more effective and powerful.

The Four-Step System

There are four easy steps to add-on selling. Every application follows the steps. You can customize it, spice it up, add to it, or vary it to a degree if you like, but it always boils down to four components:

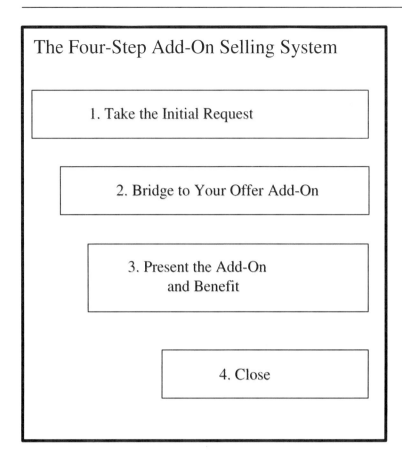

The Four-Step Add-On Selling System

1. Take the Initial Request

2. Bridge to Your Offer Add-On

3. Present the Add-On
and Benefit

4. Close

Here's a closer look at each of the components:

1. Take the Initial Request.
This could be the original order, the handling of the
initial inquiry, dealing with the complaint, etc. Let's
break it down further.

The Inbound Call. If you're an inbound rep, regardless
of whether you are in inside sales, customer service, help
desk, etc., your primary objective is to handle the customer's
initial request. It might be to place an order, it might be a
complaint or an inquiry. Whatever the case may be, handle
this first.

It makes a load of sense. The customer or prospect is calling you for some sort of aid or assistance. Deal with that first. It's their agenda that must be satisfied at this point, not yours. Rushing into an add-on before dealing with the primary objective not only dilutes the quality and effectiveness of the call, it can destroy a relationship. An add-on delivered too soon can, at best, annoy a client and, at worst, literally scare them off the telephone.

Boiled down, the critical issue in an add situation is timing Timed correctly, the add-on has a good chance of succeeding If it does not succeed, it has a better-than-average chance of not annoying the client. So be savvy and wait.

Let's emphasize this again so that there is absolutely no mistake:

> Handle the customer's demands, request, order etc., before you move on to the add-on.

The Outbound Call. The same principle holds true. It would seem obvious enough but it is certainly not always the case. If you are making a cold call and the objective is to sell, deal with that first. Once the client's needs have been identified and you have presented your solution, *close them.* Get the customer to say "yes" before you recommend the add-on. Remember that customers do not like pushy and aggressive sales reps. If you start up-selling or cross-selling too early in the process, a good deal of your clients will get turned off. They'll feel that you are simply trying to upgrade the order for your sake and not theirs. Once this state of "dissonance" is reached by your client, your goose is cooked.

It is okay, in fact it is recommended, that you *probe* for add-on opportunities. You can gauge the client's receptiveness for additional items, but don't hit them hard with it.

Timing.

It's always timing. Whether it's your golf swing, the perfect pass to the wide receiver, the backhand volley, or the add-on sale, it always boils down to timing. So time your add-on to the end of the call, not any sooner.

2. Bridge to the Add-On

You will see the "bridge" in almost every add-on situation, so get used to it right now.

The bridge is merely a transition phrase that alerts your client that you are about to provide some information. It introduces the add-on; it bridges the gap between the initial client request and your attempt to add-on. I think you've got the point, but here are a few examples:

"Ms. Allen while I have you..."

"Oh, by the way, did you know..."

"Pat, I would like to take a moment to…"

"Incidentally..."

"Before I process this..."

It's easy.

3. Present the Add-on and the Benefit

There's nothing mystical or magical here either. You simply state the add-on. Well, perhaps I am being a little too simplistic. This step in the add-on system consists of two components:

- an explanation of the add-on, and,
- the benefits of taking advantage of the add-on.

Most reps can get their hands around the explanation of the add-on. That part is easy.

The second part, the benefit, seems to be a stumbling block for most reps. For those of you who are not familiar with the concept, a benefit is the real reason why people buy or take action. A benefit is ultimately what the client derives by taking advantage of your add-on. Sometimes the benefit is tangible. For example, buying more might *save a customer money* on a per unit basis. For example,

> **"Ms. Allen, while I have you, did you know you get a price break when you order a half dozen. You are only two units away and that represents a total saving of $12.00 per box."**

The benefit is the money savings.

Sometimes the benefit is intangible. A customer might provide you market information in the form of a survey because it might lead to something down the road. Or, the customer might assist you out of the goodness of his heart. The motivator in this case is the feeling of goodwill. It makes the ego feel good to know you have helped:

> **"By the way, Mr. Ford, I wonder if you could help me out for a moment. We are trying to get a handle on what our customers really want in terms of value. If you have a moment, I would like to ask you about four questions to get a better sense of our product and how we can help improve it for customers like yourself."**

A bit wordy, perhaps, but the request is clear and the benefit is clearly implied.

Without a doubt, one of the biggest mistakes made by anyone in sales or a sales related position is the failure to concisely lay out the benefit. Some reps don't know how, but even those who do know how are often guilty of assuming their client clearly understands what's in it for them.

The hidden agenda here is that you create job aids to assist you. There is a chapter on job aids, but for now, understand that they help you present the offer. Sometimes it is a "word-for-word" script that you can use to guide you. At other times, it is a product description that explains the benefits to the client.

4.The Close

If providing a benefit is a difficult task for many reps, then asking for the sale, or asking for permission, or asking for some sort of action on the part of the client ranks a close second.

You need to ask for the add-on sale in one of two forms:
- The Direct Close, or
- The Assumptive Close.

The Direct Close. The direct close is a straight forward, no fuss, no muss approach. For example,

> *"Would you like me to add that to your offer?"*

This works exceedingly well in add-on selling situations such as an up-sell or a cross-sell. But it works well in other situations, too. For example, suppose you inquired about asking a few questions to research the market, the product, or the competition. You might close with,

> *"Would that be okay with you?"*

> *"May I proceed?"*

Some might argue that the only problem with a direct close is that while it is clear and to the point, it does set you up for an easy "no" or "I'm really in a rush". Also, experience has shown that customer service reps are generally reluctant to use this type of close. Many perceive it as too pushy.

The Assumptive Close. The assumptive close is a little easier for customer service reps and actually helps reduce rejection for almost everyone. As the name implies, the assumptive close assumes a sale has been made. As such, it does not ask for a major purchase decision, but rather asks for a minor administrative decision. For example, in a cross-sell or up-sell:

> *"I can add that to your order right now..."*

> *"We can get that out today with your initial order..."*

> *"Would the same billing address apply..."*

After this phrase has been provided, you must shut up. Let the customer ponder and determine whether it is a go or a no go.

Another way to proceed with a close like this is to simply move on and not pause. Seems contrary, but it works well in some situations. For instance,

> *"Ms. Neshevich, I want to thank you for your order and, while I have you, might I ask you about three or four questions regarding your use of our product. This will help us make modifications to help customers like yourself, get the most from the product.*
>
> *The first question is…"*

Obviously, the acceptance was assumed because the rep launched into the question phase. On occasion, this can annoy a client because it is somewhat presumptuous in nature. But the majority of times, it will be accepted, provided your add-on request is relatively short.

Summary

There you have it: a system. Four simple steps to help guide you with each add-on selling situation. When you first use the system, it may feel awkward. It's like learning to skate or ski or drive for the very first time. It's awkward because you are consciously aware of just how incompetent you are (or feel). After practice and experience you will move out of this phase into a consciously competent phase. This means you are conscious about what you are doing, and whatever you are doing, you're doing it well. Your ultimate objective is to be unconsciously competent. This is the phase where you don't have to think about performing the task. It becomes automatic.

Chapter 5

The Cross-Sell
(The Granddaddy of Them All)

In college football, the Rose Bowl is considered the "grand daddy" of the them all, which is to say that it is considered the best of the best, the number one game, the game that ranks number one during the holiday season.

It's a great metaphor for the cross-sell. If there was a Rose Bowl for add-on selling, it would be the cross-sell. It would be the "granddaddy" of all the applications if only because it is so rich in potential. "Whoa Nelly!" as Keith Jackson, the venerable college sportscaster might say. The cross-sell is not used nearly enough, but it has as much of a monetary excitement as a game between Nebraska and Oklahoma.

We'll take a very detailed look at the cross-sell in this chapter. We'll look at how to set up, which is the strategy, and how to make it work in a call, which are the tactics.

What is a Cross-Sell?
Earlier in the book I asked if you had ever been to McDonalds and ordered a hamburger. Smiling brightly, there's a good chance the server asked if you would like fries or a soda with your meal. Guess where McDonalds makes the most money? Guess which products have the greatest profit margin? You got it, fries and sodas. And as we merrily munch away, McDonalds laughs all the way to the bank.

A cross-sell is the process of adding on and selling a related, or sometimes non-related, item to complement the original purchase. And one more thing - it generates additional revenue, just in case you forgot that little point.

Where to Use Cross-Selling

Obviously, cross-selling works best in a sales situation. Whether you work on order desk like Victoria's Secret or Lee Valley Tools, or you sell face-to-face like at CSU Computers or McDonalds, you can cross-sell, provided you have thought the matter through.

Let's look at the process of cross-selling for a brief moment. I have a love affair with roller ball pens. I'm coming out of the closet and admitting it. I search for them as though each pen were the Holy Grail - a noble quest for that one perfect roller ball. (It's silly. I know it and my wife will testify to it.)

I am on every vendor's list and I buy most of them through catalogs. Typically, I call and place an order. Because many of the pens are unique or from places like Germany, France, and Switzerland, refills that actually fit are hard to find at a local business supply store. The cross-sell makes sense, particularly if I want to use the pen continuously. So, here's the point. The savvy vendor will recognize this and make cross-selling a regular part of the selling process.

But before we go further, let's deal with the number one objection that I encounter when I talk about cross-selling.

"But it Won't Work in My Business!"

It's during this point that the cynical rep or sales manager will raise his or her hand and say to me, *"Cross-selling works just fine for average little things like roller ball refills but not my product. My product is different. Unique You can't. cross-sell with my product."*

Bull.

You can.

You simply need to scratch the surface a bit. Cross-selling works in the computer hardware industry.

It works in hotels and restaurants.

It works in retail clothing.

It works when selling software.

It is powerful in the financial industry, selling everything from mutual funds to credit cards.

It's had success in selling beer to vendors and dental impressions to dentists.

It works in hospitals selling tubing with troccars (it does not matter if you know what these are - the buyers do).

I use it selling training programs, and newsletter companies cross-sell other newsletters.

E-commerce book retailers sell related books that other readers recommend. And so on.

End of story.

Why Does it Work?
Cross-selling works. Period.

The biggest reason it works is because the initial buying decision has already been made. That hurdle has been overcome. When clients have made up their minds to buy, adding on an item is relatively easy because the clients are open to spend more. They are receptive to offers that you you might have. So, in effect, the selling ground is fertile.

But there are a couple of other reasons to take into consideration. Let me ask you a question.

Why do people and companies not buy more from you or your company?

Reason 1: They don't know what more you have to offer.

Customers don't buy more from you because you haven't told them what you have.

You haven't educated them on what is available, what might complement the purchase, or what is on sale. Unless they have a flyer or brochure in their hands, how could they know? And even if you have marketing support material, such as a catalog, not everyone flips through each and every page.

The problem with many sales reps is that at some point in their career, they forget that the customer does not think about you, your company, and your product eight hours a day. This might surprise you, but customers have other things to think about.

The rep, however, thinks about the product and services daily. After a while, the average rep comes to believe that the customer should know everything you have to offer. The rep takes it for granted that the customer is aware of the entire product line. What is worse, the rep eventually plays a little mind game with himself: "Oh, if they wanted more, they'd buy more?" And with that little mantra playing, they ignore the opportunity to educate the client.

Grand and Toy, a large office products chain in Canada has learned this lesson well. Despite monthly flyers and despite an attractive catalog, the majority of buyers don't know half of what is available. People order what they need and don't always have the time to browse.

44

This is where you need to be "consultative". You need to be the customer's advisor, teacher, guide, whatever. By pointing out various items you have to offer, you'll often hear a surprised sigh that goes something like this, "Gee, I didn't know you offered that."

Here's something that might surprise you and get you over the hump about cross-selling:

Most customers want to know what you have!

We know this because they've told us. In various surveys conducted with clients, 82% of customers wanted to know the special of the month, the latest offer, items on sale, etc. (I'll be tossing that figure out every now and then, so get used to it.) Knowing this should compel you to use the cross-sell more often because it means better customer service.

Oh, and did I mention it also means better sales for you?

Personally, I am glad when I buy my roller pens and the customer service rep reminds me of refills. I like it when they tell me that the refills can't typically be bought at a Staples or Office Depot or Grand and Toy. It saves me time and hassle. I am more productive when I simply have to reach into the desk and grab a refill rather than order it and wait a week.

The Concept of Customer Share. Let's talk about an interesting marketing term. Actually, let's talk about two marketing terms.

The first is "market share". Without going into a Marketing 101 class, market share is the available market that could buy your product. Here's a simple way to look at it. Let's take the beer market, and say there are 100 million people who drink beer (that's just a figure pulled out of a hat). If your company sells beer to 25 million people, you have a 25% market share.

45

The second term is based on this principle. It's called "customer share" and it represents all the products the customer can typically buy from you. If the customer buys ten products and you sell her only one, you have 10% of the "customer's share". Your objective should be to acquire as much customer share as you can, if you can. At Grand and Toy, the client might be being paper, toner cartridges, pens, pencils, and the like, but they might be unaware that the company sells office furniture. You can grab that "share" of the customer.

I tell you this because cross-selling is a way to get more customer share. Here are three points to consider.

> 1. It is easier than marketing to new prospects because customers already know you and your company.
>
> Less education and convincing is involved.
> 2. It's also less expensive. You don't have to pump money into creating, sending and following up on brochures, letters etc.
>
> 3. Finally, it doesn't take much time. A casual mention is often all it takes.

In summary, most customers don't buy more because they don't know you have it. This is a fact and now that you know it, you're in position to leverage it with a cross-sell.

Reason 2: You don't ask.
But there is something else to consider. Something very important and in a way disturbing.

> **Customers don't buy more from you because you don't ask.**

Gee, that's a scary thought. It suggests that even if your customer knows what you have to offer, they don't buy more because they have not been asked to buy more.
It makes sense. The customer is buying one thing. Their mind is not on related items even if they are aware they exist. For instance, you know that McDonalds sells fries and soda but you came into the place with a hamburger on your mind. In this instance, the cross-sell is merely a suggestion or a reminder knowing that the customer is in a buying state of mind.

Asking for a sale is a huge part of the entire selling process. I trust that you know that by now. But sometimes reps get complacent. Heck, they have a sale in their pocket already. Break out the champagne! Why do more? The objective has been met.

You should do more for two reasons.

First, it's good for you. You sell more, you make more. You become more valuable to yourself and your company.

You become a star!

Second, it's good for the customer. Remember 82% of all customers want to be told of related items, particularly if it means savings. Cross-selling, done well, is better customer service.

You cannot sell more if you don't advise the customer and ask for the sale. I can't make it any clearer than that
Let me ask you something to put this all in perspective. I have mentioned this before.

What's the worst the customer can say?

Think about it. If you present your cross-sell, one that, of course, could possibly benefit the customer, what is the worst they can say. I'll tell you.

"No."

That's it. No big deal. Move on.

If you've presented your cross-sell politely and professionally in a consultative manner, as opposed to puking out a pitch in a fast, I-don't-give-a-darn manner, the worst the customer will say is "no".

To date, not a single rep I have met or trained has had his eyes clawed out. Hard to believe, I know, but it's true. Tongue in cheek aside, they won't mind at all when you present it well. (Good incentive to read this book from cover to cover!)

Final point: If you are still having trouble convincing yourself, then let me simply say, "GET OVER IT."

ROI: What Can You Expect

The rate of return on a cross-sell is similar to that of an up-sell. It will vary with the nature of the product/service, the skill of the rep, the discounts, etc. But generally speaking, about one in every four customers will take advantage of your offer, provided it makes sense.

The 25% rate can be higher or lower. The trick is to experiment. You never know what might sell. For example, Lee Valley Tools sells high quality gardening and home tools. Some time ago, the company purchased a quantity of make-it-yourself bird houses for the Christmas season. One rep in particular would mention the bird house at the end of every order and suggested it would make a great "stocking stuffer". She'd sell two or three in a call. About 40%-50% of everyone she spoke with would say yes. Timing, cost, the nature of the cross-sell, and the rep's enthusiastic endorsement resulted in a great cross-sell.

Does it always work this way?

No. Of course not.

However, the few extra seconds it cost to mention the cross-sell is minuscule compared to the potential return on the investment.

Eight Ways to Increase Your Odds of Cross-selling Success

If you want to increase the acceptance rate, then here are a few rules to consider.

1. The Rule of 25%

This percent has nothing to do with your expected return on investment, but everything to do with the cost of your add-on.

The value of your add-on sale should not increase the overall order by more than 25%. Let's suppose you work for Franklin Covey and you sell a time management system for $100.00. Your add-on items, such as extra files, pre-printed forms or directories, or a storage binder should not exceed $25.00.

Of course, the percentage can be less, and at times it is more. The 25% is a rule of thumb. Despite the fact that people are motivated to buy, they still have a mental limit as to the amount they will dispense. For whatever reason, experience in virtually every industry rarely exceeds 25%.

Let's look at this issue from another angle. As you increase the value of the cross-sell item, your sale moves from a simple "add-on" to a more complex "new" sale. In effect, the customer is making a whole new purchase that he or she had not anticipated. This can work from time to time because that's the most effective way to leverage the moment. Generally, it's a waste of time.

2. Don't Forget *the* Profit

The whole point of the add-on exercise is to make money. Duh! The point is, the item(s) you choose should be those where the profit margin is healthy. One reason McDonalds does well is that the margin on fries and soda is, well, huge. Leverage the moment to its financial best.

3. Don't Dump Junk

Very quickly, I will say that regardless of the margin, be careful not to "dump junk".

In other words, don't use the cross-selling opportunity to unload items that are poor in quality or stacked in inventory because no one wants them. Oh, you may get away with it in the short run. Heck, you might even get rid of your stock. In the short term, you can actually have a hay-day. In the longer term, your strategy of cross-selling will fizzle and die as your clients become more and more wary of your attempts to sell junk. They'll say no. Or worse, they won't call or visit again. You'll see this in more detail in Chapter 19, "The Dark Side".

Don't get me wrong, you can have clearance sales. If the stock isn't moving, add a huge discount and tell the client that you're clearing it. Catalog retailers have known this for years. Open any Land's End, L.L. Bean, or Victoria's Secret catalog and you'll usually find a clearance page. You can use the sample principle when speaking with a customer. Just let them know.

4. Limit the Offer

Limit your choice of cross-sell items. One, maybe two, related items is about all your customer will tolerate.

Recently, I ordered a product for my computer. The rep attempted a cross-sell on, not one, not two, not even three, but FOUR items. There was almost a desperate edge to the

tone. I found it annoying and a waste of time. This type
of relentless cross-sell tactic is precisely what customers
dislike. Don't do it.

Don't kill the goose that lays the golden egg. Exercise
some common sense.

5. Relate the Offer to the Initial Product
Cross-selling works best if your add-on product is related
to the original purchase.

Think about it for a moment. If you were to buy a printer
for your office, having a supply of ink cartridges makes
sense. There's no confusion about the relationship. It's a
good idea. Good ideas are not particularly hard to sell.
The cartridges are related to the operation of the printer.
Selling a warranty to a piece of machinery is also logical and
related. At McDonalds, fries make sense. So does a Coke.
Selling a tie with a shirt is complementary. These items
are related to the original order.

Just so you understand, selling a related item does not
require a great deal of pondering on the part of your
customer. That's the key to a good cross-sell. It should be a
relatively quick and painless thought process for your
client. It is not a complex sale, and, provided your add-on is
within the 25% range, the customer does not have to
consider budget.

I'll bet you anything that you would be hard-pressed not to
find related products/services that you could add-on.
Virtually every product has some related item.   So, the trick
is to sit down and examine the products that you typically
sell in any given day. The next step is to match the product
with related products/services. Use a job aid to make the process
easier (see Chapter 18: "Job Aids").   That's all there is to it.
(See Chapter 18: Job Aids). That's all there is to it.

By the way, if you can't find a related product or service
to add-on, it's okay. Don't worry about it. Well, hang on
a minute.

6. Sell Unrelated Items
How's that for a turnabout?

Call me twisted, but it's sometimes fun to mess with your
mind.

Rule 6 says to break Rule 5 - on occasion. The fact of the
matter is that you can sell unrelated items in some
circumstances.

"Specials." The way to position the unrelated item is to
present it as the "Feature of the Month" or "Today's
Telephone Special" or "Clearance items". At an Ottawa,
Ontario Grand and Toy outlet, sales representative, Jeff,
takes and makes calls to business clients. Every month
the store features "Jeff's Specials". These are special
items that Jeff has only for his telephone clients. They are
not advertised to anyone else. As the clients get to know
Jeff, they begin to ask "Hey what's your special of the
month?" Heck, they're cross-selling themselves.

However you state it, the customer becomes aware that it
is not related. Many will simply say they are not
interested, while others will be curious and listen.

At Levenger, a company that specializes in writing products (like roller balls), a small bean bag frog is often
suggested at the end of an order. I think it costs about ten
bucks. It's a bit whimsical, but it also has a functional use.
The company sells a lot of them by utilizing them as a way to
keep your computer mouse cords untangled and out of the way.
As I mentioned earlier, at Lee Valley Tools a birdhouse was
Recommended, which rarely relates to the items bought, but it

did relate to the Christmas season and it did relate to the "do-it yourselfer" mentality. It sold like hotcakes.

7. Promote the Cross-sell

There are ways that you can get more mileage out of your cross-sell, and one way in particular is to create awareness that cross-sells exist. For example, using mailers, faxes, and e-mails can advise clients that you have a special for the month. For example, Barnes and Noble will use something like this, which states,

---

THIS MONTH'S SPECIAL

How to Make Luck:

7 Secrets Lucky People Use to Succeed

by Marc Meyers

The mailer, e-mail, brochure, or fax makes a great pre-text for a customer service or sales reps to say,

"By the way, did you happen to see our special Book of the Month for business buyers in the flyer we sent?"

Companies that use flyers and catalogs know that many inbound calls are based on a response to the literature that has been sent. Positioning a special up front is easy to do and makes the cross-sell simpler for the rep.

If you're not doing something like this but you can, then get on board.

8. Leverage the Technology

Not everyone can do this, but many call centers can.
Whenever you place a customer on hold, run a
Message, such as:

> **"Be sure to ask for our Special of the
> month..."**

Or,

> **"Save $45% when you order the "TimeSaver
> Newsletter" this month. Sent monthly, this
> eight-page letter is full of ideas, tips and
> techniques to make you more productive.
> Ask your rep about it."**

These messages alert the customer about your cross-sell
Items, which in turn makes the selling easier. Simple stuff.
Works well. Do it.

You'll learn more about this in the chapter on "Add-On
Selling on the Internet", but you can use messages imbedded
in the text to advise the customer about certain specials.
This "fertilizes" the selling ground so that when an order
is placed, the cross-sell becomes easier.

The Four-Step Selling System to Presenting the Cross-Sell

Okay, we've looked at how to set up the cross-sell from a
strategic point of view. Let's hunker down and look at the
tactics. This is how you make the cross-sell work. It's easy
when you follow the Four-Step Process.

**Step 1: Take the original order and all the key in-
formation.** If you've been reading the book from the
front, you'll know that you always handle the customer's
initial order first.

Capture all the data required to fulfill the order and then, and only then, move on to the cross-sell. This is important to emphasize because in their anxiousness to cross-sell, some reps don't process the original order before moving on to related items. This can scare, or more accurately, annoy, the customers who might change their minds.

Tips On Taking The Original Order

Here are some ideas that can increase your success rate:

- **Compliment the customer on the original purchase.**

After the order has been taken, but before you bridge to the cross-sell, compliment the customer on their choice of product. This can help increase your chances of cross-selling a related item.

Lori Ebright is a call center supervisor for Victoria's Secret. Perhaps one of the most successful catalog companies and retailers in North America, Victoria's Secret teaches their reps to be consultative. They understand the concept of customer share and how to assist the customer in assessing other purchases.

Lori explains that complimenting a customer on their purchase creates an affinity or bond with the client. Everyone likes to feel that they have made the right choice. A Victoria's Secret customer service rep might say,

> **"Oh Sarah, that's a great choice and a really great price."**

Here are a few more examples:

> **"Oh, that's a great choice..."**

> **"Lots of callers are buying it..."**

"That's a really popular item..."

"I know you'll really like it..."

"It's one of our best sellers..."

"Everyone has been raving about it..."

"We get lots of feedback from satisfied customers..."

"I have one myself..."

This tip, tactic, technique, whatever you want to call it, has been successfully demonstrated over the years in a variety of situations.

One in particular is in the restaurant trade. Servers have known for a long time that complimenting a customer's choice of food selection results in bigger tips. There is a psychology to it. Almost everyone likes the fact that they made "the right choice" and telling them generally makes them receptive to suggestions.

- **Compliment, but compliment sincerely.**

If you cannot utter these compliments with absolute sincerity, then don't bother.

Most customers can't help but feel good and positive when they hear it from a rep who is genuinely sincere. Lori is adamant about this fact. The customer knows if the rep is pandering and false. If the complimentary message cannot be delivered with the utmost sincerity, don't use it.

If you haven't bought the item in question, don't even suggest that you have. You'll get caught and you'll get burned. If customers aren't raving about your product, don't try to fake it. It'll catch up with you sooner or later. Your tone of voice accounts for about 80% of the message, while your words represent only about 20%. What this means is that if the sincerity isn't there, if it isn't real, you'll pay a dear price.

2. Bridge to the Cross-Sell

The bridge announces the transition from the initial sale to the cross-sell. It is your way of advising the customer that you have something to add. It is your way to get their attention for another moment. That's all. Here are some examples that you have seen elsewhere in the book:

> **"Ron, by the way, did you know...."**

> **"While I have you, Mrs. Hodges..."**

> **"Mr. Llewellyn, if you have a moment..."**

At Victoria's Secret, the complimentary phrase flows into the bridge directly. For example,

> **"Sarah that's a great choice and at a really great price. By the way, since you seem to like cotton pajamas, let me show you something on page 29 that you may like."**

Just a few things with this little phrase. First, is the use of the name. When you use the client's name, they listen. It shows YOU listen. It creates a sense of rapport. People are more apt to consider your offer when there is a perceived connection.

Secondly, Victoria's Secret knows that pretty much everyone scans the catalog from cover to cover. We talked about this earlier. This technique educates the client about other products.

Finally, the rep gets the client to interact by turning to a specific page. The client can actually see the product being offered. This makes the selling process a heck of lot easier and a whole lot faster.

Learn from this.

These are just examples. Any little phrase can work; however, to emphasize, these phrases work magically well if you have prefaced them with a sincere compliment. (Just wanted to remind you.)

3. Present the Cross-Sell and the Benefit

When you present your cross-sell, your message should be short and sweet. This is not a complex selling situation. In cross-selling, you do not want to spend a lot of time "selling". Time is an important commodity for both you and your customer. Cut to the chase.

Let's go back to Lori Ebright at Victoria's Secret. The rep will provide a description of the product. For instance,

> **"These pajamas are 100% cotton and light-weight - absolutely perfect for the summer season just around the corner. They come in a variety of colors and patterns. And best of all, they are only $29.00."**

You see nothing complex. It is simple, but with enough descriptive detail to educate the client.

Just to show you that the cross-sell applies to more than simple items like clothing, at CSU, a software supplier, the cross-sell goes something like this:

> "Vince, thanks for you order. We'll get the Works package out today and you'll have it in about a day and a half."

> "Incidentally, we have the late Norton Utilities upgrade on sale this month. You save $15.00 and you get your computer working up to par. "

> "Can I add that to your order?"

The Wine Shippers in Chicago use this:

> "Ernie, you'll love the Cab-Sauv based on what my customers are saying. By the way, earlier you mentioned that you enjoy a good Chardonnay. We have a Stag's Leap that's like heaven on earth."

Notice the complimentary phrase, the use of the name, and the descriptive wording of the Chardonnay. Powerful stuff.

And here's another tip for you:

Don't supply a benefit. (How's that for a curve ball?)

Use the "Casual Mention Approach". Do you remember your English and grammar classes? There were all sorts of "rules" like "place the "i" before the "e"… Just when you figured you had mastered that, the teacher would throw out an exception to the rule, such as "i" before "e" except after "c". Well, here's the exception in the cross-sell.

Don't bother with the benefit. Simply add things like,

> "Would there be anything else with that to-day?"

"How are you fixed for copier paper and cartridges?"

These are nothing more than prompts to jog the customer's memory. They apply to products that do not require a good deal of thought. Adding a benefit to these helps improve your odds, but I recognize that it can be overkill in certain circumstances.

Step 4: The Close

The close is important. I'll beat this horse to death. Remember, we want the cross-sell to be short and sweet. The close completes the cross-sell "circle" by getting the customer to take action by making some sort of decision.

If Victoria's Secret has learned anything, it has learned that the close is important. Some customers need a gentle nudge in the right direction but, more importantly, customers need to know it is decision making time. So Victoria's Secret will use good, old-fashioned closes like,

"What color would you like?"

"The PJs are cut larger for comfort, what size would be best for you?"

If you can leverage a special offer, do so. It makes the selling a whole lot easier. For instance, when you buy a certain amount, shipping is free. This can be a powerful incentive.

"Sarah, you are only $10.00 away from free shipping. Would you like me to add that to your order."

Use closes. Use them every time.

HUGE TIP

Shut up.

Did I mention that once you have offered the cross-sell and closed, your next step should be to "SHUT UP?"

Don't say a word.

Let the customer mull over the offer and make up his or her mind.

Don't clutter the moment with additional chatter.

Summary

Cross-selling should be a regular part of your selling process. It is a way to increase sales and increase customer service. I cannot make it any plainer than that. There should be no reason whatsoever for not cross-selling.

Get started right now. Take a sheet of paper. List your three top-selling products. Beside each, list possible cross-sells. Note those that are directly related. Note those that are not. Check the prices of each. Do they fall within the 25% range? Can you discount? Can you create a "Special of the Month?"

Chapter 6

The Up-Sell

If cross-selling is the Crown Jewel of add-on selling, then the up-sell must classify as the Hope Diamond. The potential to generate additional sales, while at the same time deliver exceptional service is endless. It's not hard to implement and it is oh, so profitable.

If you haven't read the first four chapters, chances are you're a sales rep, or a keen customer service rep, or a manager who is anxious to cut to the quick and get into the nitty-gritty of selling. And that's okay. In fact, that's great. You don't have to read the first four chapters unless you're still a little queasy about applying add-on selling with your customers and prospects.

What's an "Up-Sell"?
An up-sell is the process of increasing the value of a sale by adding one more of a given *quantity* of the product. For example, you place an initial order for four boxes of copier paper, but the sales rep advises you that there is a price break if you buy six. The up-sell is two more boxes; the value of the sale has increased in about five and half seconds.

Another form of an up-sell is to upgrade the *quality* of a product. For example, you place an order for a Series 7300 laptop computer, but after some discussion with the rep, she recommends a Series 7500 because it will better meet your needs. The value of the sale is upgraded for you, and for the customer!

Either way, the up-sell is designed to increase the revenue generated by that particular sale.

Where to Use the Up-Sell

Pretty obvious, isn't it. You can use the up-sell with,

- the inbound order desk,

- outbound telesales, and,

- field sales situations.

Obviously, it can be used in any situation where buying an additional quantity of a given product makes sense.

"Not my product!"

Let's deal with the first objection I normally encounter at this point. "It won't work with my product or service." I hear the same thing with a cross-sell. Granted, not every product will lend itself to an up-sell, but there are a couple of points to consider. First, virtually any and every commodity item can benefit from the up-sell. Simple sales are ripe for the up-sell.

Second, up-sells can also apply to more complex sales, such as computers, software, vehicles, power tools, etc. It takes a more consultative rep to achieve the up-sell but it is possible. A good rep who questions effectively and accurately assesses the client's needs can, and indeed should, up-sell if it make sense.

Before you dismiss up-selling, make sure you have thoroughly looked at every possibility. Up-Selling takes some thought...and it is worth it.

Why Does It Work?

The up-sell works extremely well in many, if not most situations. And it's important that you understand why the up-sell works. Once you understand the psychology behind the process, it becomes easier to implement on virtually any order. To understand this better, let's take a look at consumer behavior relative to the buying process.

The Decision to Buy. Typically, we as consumers go through two phases when it comes to purchasing. Once we have identified a need or a want, we go through a process where we determine whether we want to buy or not. This is first phase: the *actual decision to buy.* Your customers and prospects go through this phase as well. Once they have made up their minds to buy, selling (and Up-selling) is simplified.

What to Buy. The second phase is really nothing more than a decision of *what* to buy to fulfill the particular need. The customer is in a "search" phase. He or she is looking for a solution.

What is important to understand is that your customer or prospect is in an extremely receptive frame of mind to buy additional products from you. Any sort of additional investment, provided it is not overly extravagant, is not a big hurdle in their minds because they are already primed to buy. So, the idea is to tap into this receptivity with an offer that benefits the client.

Manipulative?

From time to time, sales reps will suggest that knowing this tendency is manipulative. I disagree. You are *not* manipulating the customer. You are making a suggestion or a recommendation that might benefit the client further. You are not twisting their arm, and provided there is nothing tricky or unethical about your up-sell, then you have every right to make an offer. Arguably, the up-sell is, in fact, more consultative. Ultimately, the customer makes the decision. They have a choice.

ROI: What Can You Expect?

Everyone wants to know what kind of response rate he or she will get with his or her up-sell. In other words, if an up-sell is presented, how many will go for it?

The up-sell results depend on the nature of the product, the nature of your offer (if discounts are applied), and the nature of your reps and the training they have received. All these combine to impact the net result of your efforts. There is no single answer to this question. As a rule of thumb, 25% of your orders can be up-sold. This is the same figure for cross-selling. But it has been higher. I have seen it as high as 50%. It can be lower. I have seen an 8% up-sell rate, but the up-sell was significant enough that it blew the doors off the revenue projections. But, if you need to do the math, begin with 25% and move from there.

You really have to ask yourself a key question: even if it only worked 2% of the time, what did it cost to get that additional revenue? The answer is "peanuts." The cost of taking 15-20 seconds more time on a call is negligible compared to the return, provided you have done everything you can to prepare yourself or your people.

The Four-Step System to Presenting the Up-Sell

Remember system selling from Chapter 4? Well, here it is again for the up-sell. As I said, I am a big believer in "system selling" because it breaks add-on selling into manageable parts. Master each part and you have a system. Once you master the system, you will start generating additional revenues.

Let me say it one more time, and then I will leave it alone: I am absolutely convinced that if you have a system, and you manage the system, you can be successful in sales (and in this case, add-on selling) even if you lack what some call "natural" sales talent. If you are a talented or naturally gifted salesperson, then the system will make you even more effective.

1. Take the Original Order and All the Key Information.
When a call arrives, make absolutely certain that you get the initial order and all the vital information for shipping, handling, etc. Put it on paper or enter it into your computer. Whatever the method of recording the data, do it. The reason we do this is based on the old adage "A bird in the hand is worth two in the bush." In other words, first make sure you've got the initial order before introducing the up-sell (assuming it applies); otherwise, you might lose the opportunity.

The reason this is recommended has to do with the notion about assertive and pushy sales reps. We know this perception exists in many clients' minds, and justifiably so. You do not want to scare the customer off by suddenly upping the order and making him feel uncomfortable before you have captured the order and the data. If the customer is sensitive to your up-sell, then at least you can process the initial order. So remember that timing is key.

2. Bridge to the Up-Sell.
Once the order and other vital data has been taken, you can bridge to the up-sell. The bridge, as you may recall, is nothing more than a transition phase that alerts the client that something is being added to the discussion.

> **"Oh, by the way, Mr. Edgerton, while I have you..."**

> **"Ms. Jarvella, did you know..."**

"Mr. Ford, I should let you know..."

Bridging Tips

Here are some tips that make the bridge more effective. These are little things. By themselves, the tips I am suggesting here and throughout the book may seem insignificant. But placed together as whole, the tips help differentiate you and your add-on from the hundreds and hundreds of mediocre reps out there trying to do the same thing. So take note.

Say Thank You. After you have taken the initial order, say something like,

> **"Thank you for your order, we really appreciate your business."**

You learned this lesson when you were in kindergarten. The value of saying "thank you" has not diminished since that time. A sincere "thank you" makes your client feel good. It also makes them receptive to your bridge statement and to your up-sell. They tend to listen more carefully.

Use the client's name. When you use the client's name, they listen to the next 5-8 words very closely. It is not surprising. Our names are like radar beacons. When a client's name is uttered, it suddenly appears on our "screen" and we take note. You want the client to listen closely to your up-sell, so use his name.

Use a pause. The pause is merely a technique that is designed to compensate for the fact that the telephone is a non, face-to-face medium. Pausing for a second or two after uttering the client's name brings even greater focus to your next set of words. (By the way, you can interject a pause here and there throughout the conversation to add emphasis, and to get the listener to pay attention.)

3. Present the Up-Sell and the Benefit.

At this point, you have got the caller's attention so now is the time to present your up-sell. The up-sell add-on is interesting because it can be divided into two categories:

- quantity up-sell, and,

- quality up-sell.

And just when you thought it was safe to begin to up-sell, I should tell you that the quantity up-sell can be divided again into two categories:

- discounted, and,

- not discounted.

Let's take a close look at each.

Quantity Up-Sell – Discounted.

The quantity up-sell increases the *volume* of a purchase.

It is extremely advantageous if you have a discount associated with the quantity up-sell. Discounts work exceptionally well in commodity items where customers can buy in larger volumes. The discounted quantity up-sell is an easier sell for obvious reasons. If the customer buys more, there is a discount that lowers the cost per unit. It's Simple math.

Greg Anderson, president of Discus Dental Canada, and his sales reps have mastered and honed the concept of the up-sell. Discus sells teeth whitening products to dental firms. Thanks to his savvy approach to marketing and sales, Greg has grown the company from a two-person outfit to a multi-million-dollar business with over twenty employees.

Here is a typical approach to the up-sell used at Discus:

> **"Lesley, thank you for the order. By the way, did you know you get a price break if you order a dozen? You're only three syringes away, which makes a saving of $24.00 for the entire dozen. The shelf life is three years so it's a great investment. Should I add three?"**

The rep provides a clear explanation of the up-sell including a benefit statement regarding the saving. Simple. Easy. Clear and concise. That's all there is to it.

Let me toss out another example from New England because it adds additional perspective. It doesn't quite follow the model that I have presented, but because it is so effective, it is worth the time.

Steve Halley is a sales rep with Allstate Ply Corp, distributors of poly bags, shrink film, stretch wrap, and tape. Steve's approach to the up-sell is to tell the caller that he'd be glad to quote a price but he would also like to check with the pricing manager to determine the next price break and to assess how much could be saved at that quantity level.

The technique of asking the price manager apparently works well, and according to Steve, virtually everyone wants to hear what the savings would be. So there you have a New England perspective!

Here are some tips to help.

"Only three." Notice how the rep explained to the customer that he was *"only* three (syringes) away from a dozen." Always, always tell the customer the number of items they need to purchase in order to get the discount break. This makes the up-sell appear smaller and easier to afford.

Total Savings. In the aforementioned example, the rep did not simply state that the cartridges were $2.00 less each if the customer bought a dozen. The rep went on to provide a total savings of $24.00, which sounds significantly more than $2.00. It is vital, then, that you do your math before providing the total benefit. Having a job aid with the discounted figures handy, including the total savings, works wonders.

Watch your pace. One of the most annoying and self-defeating tendencies of many reps is to blurt out the up-sell at the speed of light. It's as though the rep wants to "get it over with." Your client will notice the rate of speed and sense your indifference. Or, chances are, he or she won't fully comprehend what you have recommended. Poor communication = poor results.

Quantity Up-Sell– Not Discounted

Not all products lend themselves to being discounted. Either there is not a margin with which to be played or a Business decision was made to not discount the product. Nonetheless, you can still attempt an up-sell provided you have a benefit.

One of the most significant examples of the non-discounted, quantity up-sell comes from Calgary, Alberta. When I first stumbled across the application I was skeptical that the up-sell could work, but Shell Canada's lubricant supervisor, Merge Gupta-Sunderji was absolutely certain. Sonja, one the more experienced order desk reps, will routinely attempt to up-sell to a case when a customer orders one-liter containers of oil, based on the fact that it is easier to ship.

> **"Bernard, you're only four liters away from a full case to 10W30. A full case makes shipping easier with less chance of damage, and you'll probably use it anyway."**

Amazingly, this works with many customers. First of all, the cost is not overly significant. Secondly, the product is such that it will move. It is not an item that gathers dust. And finally, the idea of goods being received in damaged condition conjures up images of returns and credits, not to mention clean up. It isn't worth the hassle, so why not?

Shell will also do the same with pallet orders. Pallet orders are bigger orders that are placed on 4x4 slabs of wood. Eric Strother is a master of the up-sell. Quiet, yet affable, he will regularly attempt to move the client to buy a full pallet.

> **"Marc, reviewing your order, it looks like you're only two and a half cases short of a full pallet. How about we top it off because it will make shipping easier with less chance of damage, saving you the hassle."**

I remember vividly when Eric first attempted this. We had just completed an up-sell training and the reps were back at their desks. Eric "went for broke" on the second call. He upgraded the order to a full pallet. In a week, he had achieved his up-sell quota for the month. Not all Shell's clients go for Eric's up-sells, but many do. And that's the point, isn't it? Besides, what is the worst that the client can say? They can politely say "no thanks." Big deal. Move on.

Quality Up-Sell

You can increase the value of a purchase by upgrading the quality of any given item. Typically, that means moving the client up to a higher category of product.

Upgrading to a higher quality usually requires a little more skill and persuasion on the part of the rep. It normally takes longer because additional information is required.

For instance, a while ago I was prompted to call The MAC Computer Warehouse when the new I-Macs were launched. I called an 800-line I saw in a magazine ad. It was time to change computers anyway so I dialed the number and told the rep exactly what I was looking for in terms of a computer and the I-Mac was just the ticket. I placed the order.

Here's how the rep, Matt, handled the call:

> **"I'd be glad to process that order for you Mr. Domanski and we can ship it within forty-eight hours.**
>
> **Mr. Domanski, while I have you, could I ask you a few questions to better understand your situation. I want to make sure we have the right product for you needs."**

The rep had clearly listened to my wish list for the computer and it was evident something wasn't adding up. Then Matt went back and asked me questions on the specific applications I had in mind. It took about five minutes or so. At the end he said,

> **"Based, on what you have told me, Jim (we had gotten closer by that time), I would recommend you upgrade to the G3. With the amount of word processing and graphic de-**

sign that you do, the G3 has more flexibility, more memory, and it is significantly faster. There is less chance of dealing with the hassle of freeze-ups and lost data. In addition, the I-Mac has a lot of features that I don't think you would really use if I understood you correctly. "

"Based on your configuration, the G3 is only about $1200 of an additional investment but if you focus in work and speed, the G3 will give you the peace of mind you need."

The end of the story? This book has been written on my nifty, speedy G3. It's fast. No freeze-ups. Easy. I love it. Complete peace of mind. Thanks Matt.

Here are tips on the quality up-sell.

Know your products inside and out. That means you really have to understand the difference between each category of product. Sometimes, it's simply a matter of one product having more features and gadgets than another. At other times, it is a little more complex.

Listen intently for clues. Clients, like myself, will provide you with information on how they might be using the product or service.

Probe. The real key to upgrading the quality of the order lies in your ability to question the client about how they plan to use the product or the service. If there is a discrepancy between what the client wants the product to do and what the product really can do, it is vital that you point this out. If you don't, the client will eventually see the that product doesn't work to his satisfaction. This will leave him or her disappointed, annoyed and frustrated.

4. The Close

The close is the last part of the system. It requires that you ask the client to take action.

It is important to emphasize that asking for the up-sell is vital to success. By posing the close, the client has to make a decision right there and then. The up-sell is generally an easy sell, which requires little thought, although upgrading quality can sometimes be a little more complex. Either way, asking for the sale speeds up the process.

Here are some simple phrases to close the up-sell:

"How does that sound?"

"Would you like me to proceed?"

"Shall I change the order?"

"Does that make sense to you?"

"Changing the order is no problem and I can ship that out today, okay?"

"Shall we keep it on your Visa?"

Oh, and to reiterate the huge tip from last chapter:

Shut up.

After you have asked for the sale, shut up. Don't say a single word. Let the customer digest your recommendations. One of three things will happen: First, they can say, "Yes". Yahoo. You did it.

Or, they can say "No thanks".

No big deal. Process the original order.

Or, they will have some sort of question/objection, which usually relates to your up-sell (price, product, whatever). Answer it and close.

Summary

The up-sell is a great way to increase revenues and it is not particularly hard to implement. Follow the four-step system, practice it, and then apply it. Finally, watch your sales soar.

Chapter 7

Converting Inquiries Into Sales

What if you could close 30% of all the inquiries you receive? Would that be of any benefit?

That's what this chapter is about: closing more inquiries. It's a short chapter. Easy to read. Easy to learn. I won't clutter the issue any further. Read on and grow rich!

What is Meant by "Converting an Inquiry Into a Sale?"

I think the title explains, it, but to make sure that we are all singing from the same hymn page, converting an inquiry means taking someone's request for information and closing them. Typically, this means a "sale" where revenue is generated.

However, "sale", might also refer to getting the inquirer to take further action. For example, it could mean having the inquirer accept a catalog or brochure, having them visit a website, or having them come into a showroom or retail environment. I call this a sale because it could potentially move the client further down the sales cycle, getting them one step closer to actually buying.

Where to Use Inquiry Conversion?
At the risk of being somewhat obvious, converting an inquiry applies to order desks, inquiry lines, help desks, information lines, reservation call centers, and inside sales groups to name but a few. You can convert an inquiry to a sale in virtually any situation where prospects or customers have questions or require information.

Can it apply to *you*, *your* business, *your* call center, with your sales or customer service staff? Absolutely. Let me ask you, if you were able to close, say, 10%, 15%, or maybe 30% of your current inquiries, what would it do for your bottom line?

Interested? Hope so. It's an easy sell.

Why Does it Work?
Here's what's important for you to know. The TARP Institute in Washington, D.C. spent years examining the importance of customer service in marketing and sales. They discovered that three different kinds of "non-order" calls existed:

1. 30% of non-order calls were "pre-purchase calls," i.e., the prospect is looking for information so that a purchase can be made

2. 40% of calls were questions on how to use a product; the customer did not understand how the product worked.

3. 30% of calls were of the "It's-broke-now-what-do-I-do?" variety.

So, big deal?

Here's the big deal. TARP discovered that of those 30% pre-purchase calls, over sixty went out and purchased that product. Translated: these were primed and motivated prospects.

Sixty percent!

If you have an inbound call center and you take inquiries, please take a moment and do the math. Suppose you have 100 inbound inquiries per day. Of those, 30 are in a pre-purchase mode. At least 18 of those 30 will eventually buy. You've got some hot prospects on the line. You can convert them. And what it's really saying is, "Thar's gold in them thar calls."

Think about this for a moment. You or your company has invested significant time and money to generate a call from a prospect or a client. It might have been letter, a brochure, a catalog, a radio or TV ad, a website, or a bill-board off the freeway. Whatever. But someone has picked up the phone and called (or perhaps dropped by for a visit).

What does this tell you? It tells you that their interest is *high*. Something inside the client motivated him or her to pick up a telephone, dial the number, let it ring and speak with a rep on the other end of the line. They've raised their hand and said, "Hey, I'm interested."

Clearly, the same rule applies here as it does in cross-selling and up-selling: *the decision to buy has been made,* or it is, in the very least, the decision to buy is in the process of being made. If we know this, then converting that interest into action is not a great leap of faith.

Here's another reason why it works: it saves the inquirer time and hassle. Many times, callers will phone around looking for the best price or availability. A certain portion of the time, you will be the first place they call, in which case, they'll call a few other places. But a certain portion of the time, you'll be the third or fourth or sixth place they've called. They've hunted. They know just about all they should know. At this point, they are likely to buy. Asking them for the sale at that moment makes the buying process easy. Provided your price is in the right neighborhood compared to the other calls that have been made, chances are, you'll get it.

Two Steps to Converting Inquiries

The Four Step system I talked about in the previous two chapters is whittled down to just two steps. What could be easier?

Step 1: Handle the Initial Inquiry

This step is identical to Step 1 in cross-selling and up-selling. Always handle the inquiry first. This means providing the customer with the information they want up front. It satisfies their immediate need. If you don't answer the question or give the information, the callers get annoyed. They feel you are being evasive, or that you are inexperienced or inefficient. So, if you have this step straight in your mind, the second step is a breeze.

Ask if they want to book it. Ask if you can take their order. Ask if you should place it on their Visa or Mastercard. It's that easy. There's no "bridge" involved this time. It is not necessary. Go for the gold. Here are some examples:

> **"Can I book that for you?"**

> **"We take Visa, Mastercard or American Express. Which would you prefer?"**

> **"How many do you need?"**

> **"How would you like those shipped?"**

> **"What size would you like?"**

"What is your shipping address?"

"Shall I put that on your account?"

I need to tell you a story to help illustrate this more clearly and to highlight a couple of tips. Not long ago, in early February, I called a few hotels in Toronto regarding a trip I had planned for my family during the spring break. With visions of visiting the Hockey Hall of Fame, Wayne Gretzky's restaurant, and catching a Leafs or Raptors game dancing in my head, the objective of my calls was simply to determine if rooms were available between March 15-18, and to get the rate. I had plenty of time, so there was no real need to make a decision at this point. I thought I'd share the info with my wife and kids and let them decide.

I called three hotels in the downtown core. The typical response to my inquiry was this:

"Yes, we do have availability on those dates at the rate of $185.00/night."

The prices varied with each but the words were almost identical, as though the reps had attended "Reservationist University" where they were all taught "Handling Inquiries 101." Arguably, the responses were good. They fulfilled my request for information in a very efficient manner. I served up the inquiry and they lobbed back the information. Ball in my court. It happens hundreds of times a day at each of these hotels.

Here's the key point: *the ball was back in my court.*

It was left up to **me** to close the sale. I had to make the decision on my own.

Instead of returning the ball and making a reservation, I decided to call a couple more hotels on the list. What the heck, may as well check them out since I've gotten this

far. I called the Cambridge Suites and spoke to the reservation
rep, Lynn. Here's how she responded to my inquiry

> " **Yes we do have rooms available March 15-18
> at a rate of 199.00 per night."**

At this point, it was obvious that Lynn was a graduate of
Reservation U. But clearly she was a grad student because
here's what she said next.

> **"It's a beautiful, one bedroom suite so there's
> lots of room for you and your family; gives
> you some space. There's an in-room mini
> fridge and microwave for snacks and a couple
> of TVs so you won't be fighting for the
> controller. Would you like me to book it for
> you?"**

Guess what?

The Cambridge got the business even at a higher cost. I
should say, *Lynn* was the one who got the business because
she asked for it.

This type of "call center volley" occurs every day of the
year in hundreds of call centers. The customer asks and
the call center provides. And while some business is
generated as a result of this volley, it is not nearly what
it could be .

Five Ways to Help the Inquirer Buy Now
1. Beef up the close with benefits.
Lynn got the sale because she asked for it. By that time, I
had a price range, the decision to buy was made. I did not

really want to dial again and wait on an ACD for three minutes to simply save a few bucks. But, she also got the sale because she "helped me buy." Look at her comments again. She and I clicked when she talked about space. Being cramped for four days in a small room has the effect of making the vacation rather crowded and confined, which makes it more stressful than restful. The mention of the two TVs and not fighting for the controller hit a chord. Stuck in the same small room with one TV has its problems. She helped me to buy by presenting the benefits that a one-room suite provides.

2. Use your voice to convey the **real** *message.*

It was not so much what Lynn said that helped me buy, but rather *how she said it.* When she talked about the room, I *felt* the spaciousness. I believed the room to be *beautiful.* The bit about the fridge, microwave and snacks had an " *insiders feel"* to it, as though she's been there, done that. This tip not only applies to converting inquiries. It applies everywhere.

3. Create a sense of urgency.

Use this tip only when it applies. In situations where you have only a few items remaining, state it up front. For example,

> **"Yes, we do have the Langeuille Knives available for$49.95 for a half dozen. It looks like there only four sets left. Shall I place your order?"**

This works well for those callers who are not quite certain, and need a little push to persuade them. The fear of missing out on something can be a powerful motivator.

Some reps object to this type of approach. Look at it another way. Suppose you don't tell your caller that there are only four sets left. The caller waffles and decides to call you back later that day or later that week. You inform her that you're out of stock. End result? Disappointment by the customer, a lost sale for you. No one wins.

But take it a step further. What if the customer somehow discovered that you knew there were only four sets left and you did not bother to tell him. Had he known, he would have acted right away. The disappointment can easily change into annoyance or anger.

4. Position the product with a sense of value.

By positioning the product, I simply mean providing a remark or two that makes the potential buyer feel that the product *is a good buy*. For example,

> **"The 'Profiting By Phone' book is available and I have to say it is selling like hotcakes. Would you like to place an order?"**
>
> **"The Works software is in stock and it is only $595.00. Shall I put that on your account."**
>
> **"Yes, we do have the Voice Shaping Tapes. I use them myself and they're great. How many do you need?"**
>
> **"Wow, you're the 20th call I've had today on this. How would you like to pay for it?"**

People like to feel or know that they are locked on to something popular. It's called "acceptance" and "approval."

How to Make the Call More Profitable

Add an add-on!

Here's where things get really interesting. Once you have asked for the sale and the inquirer says "yes," you now have a sale. You are in an order desk mode. The client is in a receptive mood for a suggestion which means a cross-sell is perfectly legitimate.

Here's another example. After an inquiry becomes a sale, you can gather market intelligence. You might ask where the caller got your number to check the effectiveness of your marketing and advertising. You might gather information about your product - what customers think or what they would like to see.

How about this: generate a lead for other products or services? You'll see this later on in the book.

The possibilities are endless. You can and should leverage the opportunity.

Summary

I told you the chapter would be short. No point in beating it to death. Converting an inquiry is that easy.

Chapter 8

Converting a Cancellation

Don't you just hate it when one of your customers cancels an order, a subscription, or a policy?

Hurts, doesn't it?

Cancellations are a part of the selling process. We know that. We accept it. But what would happen if you could reduce the number of cancellations? What would be the impact if you could convert a cancellation back into a sale?

This chapter is about converting those nasty, little cancellations into sales. You don't have to accept your current cancellation rate as "the cost of doing business." You can keep more of your customers.

Interested?

Cancellation Conversion Defined
The best way to describe a cancellation is with a straightforward example. In the first example, a customer calls and cancels his insurance, his subscription, his membership, or his order. Dutifully, the customer service rep gathers the information and terminates the relationship.

End of story.

End of money.

All the time, effort, and money used to acquire that customer is now flushed down the toilet.

Bye-bye.

A cancellation is where you have "the bird in the hand" but you let it slip away "to the bush." A cancellation is an existing source of revenue that dries up. A cancellation is the end of a relationship. A cancellation is bad news.

But the story does not have to end that way…at least not all the time. Converting a cancellation means taking a proactive approach to the situation and then attempting to save or to salvage as much of the sale as possible.

How do you do that? It's a two step process:

>First, you have to know why the client is cancelling.

>Second, you have to know the steps to take that can convert the cancellation.

Where Does It Apply?
There are two types of situations where the cancellation applies.

Continuous Flow Products and Service
The first situation where converting a cancellation can apply is where there is a "continuous flow" of goods or services to a customer. Here are some examples of what I mean:

- Subscriptions to newsletters, wire services, magazines and other publications.

- Memberships to clubs, associations, special interest groups, charities, etc.

- Services, such as insurance, lawn care and the like.

A cancellation of one of these products or services can have a significant impact. First and foremost, it means the end of a steady and continuous cash flow. That stings. Secondly, it is the end of a relationship. Some subscribers may have purchased your product for years and years.

For instance, I have been a member of the automobile association (CAA/AAA) for 20 years. Thirdly, you lose the LTV (the life time value) of that client. In other words, you lose future revenues. And finally, you have to go out and find another client to replace the lost client, and this takes time, money and effort.

One-Time Cancellations
The second situation occurs when a customer calls and cancels an order that has just recently been placed. This often happens within hours or days of the initial order and could apply to virtually any product or service. Both cancellations hurt. But it is the continuous flow products and services that really take their toll on an organization.

So, what's the ROI? The return on investment is a tough question to answer, but various surveys seem to indicate about 30% of cancellations can be converted. It's higher in some areas. For instance, we'll see an example from Australia where the cancellation rate was reduced by 50% for a subscription service.

Whether it is ten, thirty or fifty percent, you do the math. Not bad, huh?

Three Reasons Why Customers Cancel
As I mentioned a moment ago, the trick to converting a cancellation is to understand why customers cancel in the first place. Once you understand the possible reasons, you are now in a position to be more proactive in your approach. There are, in fact, three reasons why customers cancel:

- Dissatisfaction with the product or service.

- The product or service no longer applies or is no longer needed.

- Buyer remorse.

Let's take a closer look at all three:

Reason 1: Dissatisfaction with the Product/Service

You can find more on this topic in Chapter 10, "Selling on a Complaint" and in Chapter 17 "Down-Selling", but let's get started here. Some customers cancel because of some sort of dissatisfaction with a product or service. It could be price, performance, or a lack of service…heck, it could be any number of things.

For example, when I purchased a cell phone, I scanned the market, but, quite honestly, I did not do a very thorough job. But based on some compelling and persuasive advertising, I chose a well-known company (who shall go nameless) and made the purchase by telephone.

The word "disappointment" does not even come close to the experience.

Two events: First, the sexy little unit would not work when I stuck the chip inside. Oh, to be sure, I called the company and the rep took me through a step-by-step diagnosis only to inform me that it was a faulty chip. The solution was for me to drive across town to their retail location and get a new one. Or send the other one back, at my expense, and have a new one sent to me.

Well, I took the drive. It cost me a couple of hours, but I did it. The phone worked. Hurrah. Or, so I thought. The next week, I was in Vancouver and Portland and I called my office from the airport. I got some quirky message that said there was no service. Gee, maybe the West Coast is a "no cell zone". Heck, I didn't know. But it did not work in Toronto or Cleveland. Fed up, I called the carrier and cancelled. The rep politely took the information and cancelled the service.

While the story is a bit belabored, there are a couple of dynamics at work here that are handy to understand if you hope to effectively convert a cancellation.

Customers Rarely Tell You Why. Here's another little lesson in consumer behavior. When customers do have a problem or complaint, the vast majority don't tell you. That's right. They don't tell you. They don't tell you for three reasons:

- They don't think you really care,

- they don't think you can help, and,

- they don't like the hassle.

We'll look at these reasons in depth in the chapter on "Selling on a Complaint", but for now, simply understand that one of these little things is going on in the customer's mind. If you don't get them to open up, you'll never have the opportunity to show that you care, that you can help, and that you don't think it is a hassle.

But the real crux of the matter is, customers often cancel because of minor dissatisfaction that builds up in their mind. Very, very often, the problem can be solved quickly and easily. Ask yourself, how often does this happen to you or in your business? How often does a customer call in and cancel, and you simply let it happen? You don't ask?

Reps Rarely Ask Why. Okay, so we know that customers don't often tell us why they are cancelling. Fine. They have their reasons. But the entire issue is compounded by the fact that customer service reps and order takers rarely ask why the customer is cancelling. Maybe it's because they don't care, or maybe they don't like the hassle. More probably, they have never been taught to ask, much less solve the problem. Regardless, what this really means is that by not asking, you will lose the business. It will cost you money.

That's precisely what happened with me and the cell phone. I am not certain of the precise logic or process behind the situation, but for whatever reason, the cell phone company nor I hadn't programmed the roaming feature. Call me inept, but I learned this later when I got another phone from a competitor.

Had I explained the situation to the rep or had the rep asked me why, the cancellation would not have occurred (provided the rep could have solved the problem). But you can see the two dynamics at work. A double whammy and the cell phone company lost my business.

Reason 2: The Product/Service No Longer Applies
The second reason why customers cancel is because the product or the service no longer applies to their situation. Sometimes this is not avoidable. For instance, many families with young babies subscribe to a diaper service. For two or three years, or whatever length of time, the diapers are needed. But, at some point, little Craig and Kevin grow up and don't need diapers any more. End of service - the product no longer applies.

Sometimes, maybe even many times, the cancellation is avoidable. To help illustrate this point, we need to zip down to Sydney, Australia, and meet Patrick Hennessy. Patrick works for a company that sells business book summaries to busy executives. From time to time, they have subscribers who call and cancel because the service "no longer applies…" Busy executives subscribing to an executive book summary is not like a diaper service. The busy executive continues to be busy. Knowing that, Patrick scratches the service to determine if the product no longer applies or if there is another possible reason.

We'll come back to Patrick a little later on.

Reason 3: Buyer Remorse

The final reason why people cancel an order is because of buyer remorse. If you have ever taken a consumer behavior course, you probably ran into this term. It refers to the process that some buyers experience after they have made a purchase. They begin to regret their decision. Sometimes, they think they were too impulsive. Others think, or discover, they have paid too much. Others get into trouble with a spouse or a parent. Others just feel guilty. There are dozens of reasons, and most of them are emotional in nature.

Buyer remorse happens at the business-to-business level too. More often than not, a cancellation occurs shortly after an order has been placed. Business buyer remorse differs somewhat from consumer buyer remorse. Usually when a business cancels an order, they either have found a better better alternative, a budget has been cut, circumstances have changed, etc. The point is, it is less emotional than consumer buyer remorse.

Because it is less emotional, the opportunity to convert this buyer is greater. The trick, as ever, is to determine what caused the cancellation. Once you have that piece of information, you may, or may not, be able to salvage the order.

The Four-Step Process to Converting a Cancellation

So, now you know why customers cancel. You know why they won't tell you and you know how important it is to find out the reason for the cancellation. Here's how you do it. You can use the same process for converting a cancellation as you use with the other add-on applications. There are four relatively simple steps.

Step 1: Take the Initial Cancellation

The same rule applies for cancellations as with other add-on applications. You handle the initial request to cancel. For instance,

> **Customer:** *"I am calling to cancel my subscription."*

> **Rep:** *"Oh, I'm sorry to hear that. Let me get some information from you."*

There are some important points here.

First, note the comment of regret:

"Oh, I am sorry to hear that."

When delivered sincerely, the client has tendency to be more receptive to any questions you might have or any suggestions you might make. Moreover, if your client is dissatisfied with the product or service, your remark of regret can ease the tension. The customer begins to realize that maybe, just maybe, they have someone who really cares. (Remember: some customers don't open up to you because they don't believe you really care. This is your first step to show them that you do.)

Second, get the information. Gather all the relevant information about the customer and the account before you do anything else.

DO NOT ATTEMPT TO QUESTION THE CUSTOMER AT THIS POINT.

Your objective is to get their name, address, account Number, and any other relevant information.

At this point, I may get an argument from trainers, sales managers, consultants and others. Many might suggest that you should immediately ask the customer, "Was there a problem?" or "May I ask why?" I believe these questions are premature. Timing is everything. You need to first demonstrate to the client that you are being helpful If you begin launching into your questions at this stage, there is a good chance the customer will revert to being defensive. Chances are, they will feel a little (or a lot) uncomfortable or awkward about cancelling in the first place. It is vital, then, to show your willingness to help.

But, there is another reason. By obtaining and storing the customer data in your computer, you can get a glimpse of who and what you are dealing with. If a customer has been insured by your firm for the past fifteen years and is suddenly pulling his home, auto, and personal life insurance from your brokerage, you have a big issue. You have equity in this client. He or she probably represents significant equity in your firm. If nothing else, this information alerts you to the value of the client. Suppose that a customer calls to cancel her subscription to your $299 per year *Etiquette Newsletter* and you discover that she has been a charter member since 1992. Another valuable client! Why is she leaving?

Let's put another spin on it. The person who is cancelling his order is a first time buyer. They are still valuable because of the time your company spent to get the order in the first place, and because of the potential value this customer might have in the future.

Where this data becomes important is in Step 2: The Bridge. You can leverage the information you have reviewed to get the customer to listen. In the meantime, here is an important tip:

Listen to the customer's tone of voice. The tone can give you clues about the customer's mood or attitude. If there is an edge to the voice or if they sound angry, there is a darn good chance that the cancellation is due to dissatisfaction. This simply tells you to tread carefully.

Step 2: The Pre-Text Bridge
Once you have the information in front of you, your next step is to bridge into the inquiry phase. Above, I told you that you can leverage the information you discovered in your database.

I call this a "pre-text bridge." A pre-text is nothing more than an excuse or the reason for a remark. Here's how the pre-text bridge could look in the three scenarios described above.

> **"I have the information on your policy, Mr. Beech. Gee, I see here you have been insured with us for over 15 years and it covers your car, your company, and your life insurances. That's a long, long time. May I ask why you are cancelling?"**

There are really two parts to the bridge. The first is the pre-text. In this case, the pre-text is the fact that the person has been insured with the brokerage firm for fifteen years. This pre-text helps "soften" the client to any idea or suggestion you might want to make.

The second part of the bridge is the question itself: "May I ask why you are leaving?" The pre-text sets up the question. Fifteen years IS a long time. Most clients would feel a natural obligation to listen simply because of the longevity of the relationship.

In the second scenario, the bridge might look like this:

> **"Ms. Sopa, I was just looking at the database
> and I see you are a Charter Member since
> the newsletter began in 1992. Obviously, you
> are an important customer to us and we'd
> hate to lose you. May I ask why you are
> cancelling?"**

The pre-text was the remark about the charter membership
with a little bit of ego added. By emphasizing the fact that
Ms. Sopa was a "Charter Member" and that she was an
important customer, is flattering. Who wouldn't listen?
How could you not respond?

In the last example, we have a single order. The rep might
take this approach.

> **"Dr. Haren, I have retrieved your invoice, and
> I see this is the first time you have placed an
> order for a TENS unit with us. Dr. Haren, we
> really do value your business and we'd hate for
> your first experience to be negative.   May I ask
> why you are cancelling?"**

It is simple and easy to make the first time buyer feel special
too. The little pre-text phrase of being a first time buyer and
the "we really do value your business" can do wonders to get
the client to open up.

NEVER, ever forget, they think you don't care. They
don't think it is worth the hassle. You have to show them
that you care and that this is NOT a hassle.

TIP: Watch your tone. Your tone conveys about 80%-
84% of your message. The words that you use only represent
16%-20% of the message. If your tone is not absolutely
sincere and helpful, the words you use will be next to
useless. There has to be a note of genuine regret, otherwise
the customer will simply assume the rep is "just going

through the motions." If you can't deliver the bridge sincerely, don't bother doing it. Do it right or not at all.

Step 3: Question and Present Your Solution:
The third step starts off with a simple instruction. Here it is, once again:

SHUT UP

Once you have asked why they are cancelling a policy, a Subscription, or an order, don't say another word. The ball is in the customer's court. Tune in and listen to what she or he has to say. Remember, you are trying to determine if your customer is cancelling

- because of dissatisfaction,

- because the product/service no longer applies, or,

- because of buyer remorse.

Let's look at each of the scenarios.

Dissatisfaction. My State Farm insurance broker and I play senior men's hockey on Sunday mornings with other businessmen in the area. Before and after the games are great times to chat about our prowess on the ice and occasionally about business. He explained on several occasions that rarely does a month go by without one of his clients calling to cancel their home or auto insurance.

He follows the Four-Step approach:

"Sure Joan. I'll cancel that for you. Let me get the file."

After reviewing the file, Gary will make a remark such as,

"Gee, Joan you've dealt with me for five years now. Can I ask you why you are cancelling?"

Invariably, the Joans of the world claim to have discovered a better rate and/or better coverage. Translated, this means dissatisfaction with the rates or the coverage that Gary is providing. His next step is to say,

"Joan, I want to make sure you are doing the right thing for the right reason. Let me ask: are you certain that the coverage you are getting from ABC Brokerage is exactly the same as you have now? Would you let me review that real quick, and if anything, you'll have the peace of mind knowing for sure?"

In many circumstances, Gary will discover that the liability coverage is less or that the deductible is significantly higher or that some coverage is omitted or reduced.

Of course, the trick here is simple. You need to be savvy enough to know why people cancel. Usually, there are one or two reasons that are predominant. Once you discover these reasons, you can zero your questioning to those areas. In Gary's case, he knows that if a competitor is going to reduce a rate by a significant amount, something in the policy has to take a hit. It's as simple as that. So he probes.

A couple of things happen as a result of this type of approach. First, the customer tends to be grateful that they were informed of the variance. It sheds a whole new light upon the competitive broker. Some clients see Gary as a hero. Secondly, if the customer still feels the drop in rate is worth the reduced liability or whatever, Gary has the opportunity to re-quote at a lower rate. This means less hassle for the client in flip-flopping policies.

2. The Product/Service No Longer Applies
Okay mate, let's go halfway around the world to Australia and revisit Patrick Hennessy at Vision Publishing.

Vision publishes book summaries for executives and reviews books on leadership and books on sales and marketing. The product is designed for busy executives who simply don't have the time to read a complete book. The summary condenses the book to about eight pages. It's a time saver.

From time-to-time, subscribers call Vision to cancel their subscription. It is not because the product is unsatisfactory. It's excellent. The customer is happy. But the product is no longer doing what it should: saving the customer time.

Patrick questions to determine the reason for the cancellation. Like Gary at State Farm, Patrick knows why most executives cancel, so he is prepared for the call whenever it should arrive at his desk. Over the years, he has learned that there are two prime reasons for cancelling: content or time. As a result, he begins the process of saving the cancellation, which looks like this:

> **"I have your file here Mr. Davies. I see that you have been a subscriber for the last three years and we would hate lose you. Let me see if I can better understand this: are you cancelling because of content or because of time?"**

Customer: "Time. I just don't have the time to read the eight pages"

Ironically, a product that is designed to save time is actually costing the client money. But Vision recognizes that even an eight-page summary of two or three books re-quires time and effort to read. This is when Patrick will suggest the following.

> **"Mr. Davies, I understand. We have heard that from many executives like yourself. Let me ask you, do you drive to work?"**

> "Yes."

> **"How long of a commute is that?"**

> "45 minutes."

> **"Here's something you might wish to consider: We offer the summaries on tape. That means you can be current with the latest trends on leadership and marketing without have to take time away from your work and family. Since you're stuck in traffic, this would be an excellent time to get caught up."**

Let's look at the other reason why customers cancel: the content. The summaries have two main topics - leadership and sales and marketing. Generally, these two topics go hand-in-hand with top executives. But Vision has learned that some execs get overwhelmed with material that doesn't precisely apply to them. For instance, a CEO might find that the leadership books apply more to his needs then the sales and marketing summaries. Hence, the sales and marketing books no longer apply. She cancels. When questioned by Patrick if she is cancelling because of time or content, the executive might say:

Customer: "Content. So much of the material that is sent just doesn't apply."

> **"I understand. Let me ask you: do the summaries on leadership meet your needs?"**

Customer: "Yes. They're great."

> **"Based on what you have told me, here's what we can do. We can focus your summaries on leadership and eliminate the material on marketing and sales. This will not only keep you abreast of leadership trends but reduce the cost of your subscription. How does that sound?"**

Results?

The proof is in the pudding. Patrick and Vision will, on average, convert 50% of those who cancel. Fifty percent! Those are impressive numbers. True, some of them are reconverted at a lower rate, but that is hardly the point. The point is, a long time customer has been retained. It also means that opportunities to up-sell or cross-sell in the future remain.

3. Buyer Remorse

Buyer remorse is a little more difficult to handle if only because the customer will not always articulate that he or she feels guilt or remorse about a purchase decision. Buyer remorse refers to a situation where the customer regrets the purchase decision. It can be caused by any number of things. For instance, a husband buys a brand new rod and reel with tackle for a couple of hundred bucks. As he drives home, he begins to feel guilty because the purchase has thrown the household budget out of whack. Sometimes, the consumer will buy a product on impulse and then discover that he really doesn't need the item. It can be anything. The point: it is not an issue of dissatisfaction with the product or the service, nor is it an issue about the product being no longer applicable.

The trouble is that most customers don't pick up the phone or walk into a store and say, "Hey, I really made a mistake here. I changed my mind." They won't say, "Hey, I really messed up our budget," or "Boy, did I get in trouble at home with this purchase, so I am returning it." Some will, but most won't. And therein lies the difficulty. You won't know it is buyer remorse unless they hit you over the head with it.

The best thing you can do is follow the Four-Step Process as described. Gather the information and then use whatever bridge you choose. If the customer says something like, *"Gee, I thought it over and just decided it wasn't right for me,"* or words to that effect, chances are, you have someone who is experiencing buyer remorse. Because it is an emotional issue, you have to tread carefully. Use subtle questions such as,

> **"I understand Ms. Fawcett. Was there something about the style (size, quality etc.) that was of concern to you?"**

Your objective is to get the customer to open up. The customer may have a question or a concern that, if answered or addressed, may get to stick with their order. If so, you are in a position to fix it. For instance, if the customer were to tell you that they bought the item on impulse and that it wasn't quite in the budget, you might be able to offer a financial option.

> **"I hear where you are coming from. I see you
> purchased the bedroom set on your Visa. Did
> you know that we have zero percent financing
> and a no-payment options for 12 months?"**

In this example, you are offering a solution that might
take away the remorse by meeting thc client's needs.
This is a much more consultative approach and one that
tends to garner the customer's respect. Another strategy
is to offer an alternative product at a lower price. You'll
see more on this in the Down-Selling chapter.

TIP: If the customer circumvents the question or is vague
in his reply, DON"T PUSH IT. There is nothing, and I
mean nothing, worse than a nagging rep. The hard sell
approach to objections will do you more harm than good.
You won't convert them.

Step: 4: Close

Just to bring formal "closure" to the Four-Step Process,
the final step is to close the sale, i.e., get the customer's
commitment. If you have been reading the book from the
beginning, you will know why this is important. But if
you've jumped ahead, let me just say that asking for the
sale speeds up the process. The add-on sale is meant to be
relatively quick and painless. Don't drag it out by hoping
the customer will take the initiative.
Here are some examples:

> **"Joan, now that we've reviewed your policy,
> I can sign you up at the lower rate with less
> liability or I can keep you at the same rate
> with the higher coverage. Which would you
> prefer?"**

"So, Mr. Davies, can I sign you up for the leadership book summaries at the lower rate?"

"Ms. Fawcett, would you like the set with the zero percent financing?"

The close is so simple, so fundamental, so logical that it astounds me when so many sales reps ignore it. Sure, some of your customers will see the logic in your offer and they won't need you to close the sale. But many won't. So close the sale and make sure that you are covering your bases.

Summary

Converting a cancellation is one heck of a way to save money. Don't accept a cancellation at its face value. Follow the Four-Step Process and explore why the customer is cancelling. Determine if you can make an alternative offer or solve a problem or tackle an objection or a concern.

Chapter 9

Selling on a Complaint

*"Selling on a complaint! Have you gone mad? People
don't buy when they're angry."*

Invariably, this is the kind of response I get from sales
reps, customer service reps, and their supervisors and
managers. But the simple fact of the matter is that, indeed, you CAN and you SHOULD attempt to sell on the
complaint call. Just to make myself clear, not all
complaint calls lend themselves to a sales opportunity.
Some complaint calls are just too sensitive. But some calls
can be converted…provided you follow a couple of steps.

In this chapter, we'll first look at some compelling reasons
why you can sell on the complaint call. Next, we'll examine
the techniques that you can use to convert anger to sales.

The Opportunity

On the surface, you wouldn't think an irate customer who
is making a complaint would make a likely sale target.
But interestingly, they make great prospects. This has
been investigated, probed, examined and detailed by the
TARP Institute in Washington, D.C. TARP, a research
company, has done significant research into customer
service and the need for businesses to have a dialogue
with its customers, particularly through vehicles such as
toll-free 800-lines and e-mail.

Most Loyal/Most Valuable

Here is some compelling evidence that clearly defines the opportunity. First of all, TARP revealed that the majority of those who complain are typically more upscale and educated. Secondly, they revealed that these clients are not only more loyal but tend to be two-to-three times more valuable in terms of selling power.

This little insight is heady stuff. If you know this going into a complaint, then you'll know that by satisfying their concerns, you'll actually be SAVING a customer and your future sales. With just a little imagination and effort, you'll also know that you can take this one step further and actually SELL to them on the call.

Buy More

TARP stunningly revealed that angry customers have a propensity to buy. Why? One reason is because they already tend to be strong purchasers of your product. The other reason is that they are looking for satisfaction. Once they get it, they are happy. The buying mode kicks in again.

TARP studied a number of companies throughout the U.S. and Canada and showed that for product complaints over $100 in value, 54% of unhappy customers will buy again if their complaint is resolved. If, and here's the clincher, the complaint is solved quickly, 82% of unhappy customers will buy again.

Cross-Selling

I love the TARP guys. They're so thorough. They took their research a step or two further. They examined unhappy customers who would buy OTHER products and services offered by the company if their complaint was satisfied. For instance, in the financial services sector, 80% of those surveyed would buy OTHER products and services if their complaint was handled well. In the high-tech and telecommunications industry, 93% said they would buy other products and services.

Gee, if I were a customer service manager or a sales manager, I'd be salivating at the thought of cross-selling. If I were a sales manager, I'd be picking up the phone and calling the customer service manager and setting up a big, fancy lunch so I could employee his customer service reps to act as "sale reps."

Makes Dollars and "Sense"
All this makes perfect sense.

You see, the true test of a company is not in its ability to sell a product or a service, but rather its ability to respond to a complaint. It's when there is a problem with a company that the "rubber hits the road". If the company stands by its customer and resolves the issue, purchasing more is a heck of a lot easier. Why? Because the company stood by the customer when things were tough. It's only at crunch time that a true measure of a company is revealed.

It goes beyond cross-selling. With a little imagination you could create add-on selling opportunities for the following situations:

- Converting discontinued products to new sales,

- selling products to solve the problem (e.g., more memory for the computer),

- pre-purchase an up-sell,

- getting back the lost and inactive customer,

- generating a lead for other products/services, and,

- getting a referral.

Unhappy customers who become delighted with you tend to see you more favorably. They are more receptive to any idea or suggestion or add-on because their needs have been met.

Furthermore, unhappy customers who have their complaint resolved tend to feel obligated to you. You read that right. They feel a sense of obligation. There is a great book you've got to get that can give you more details on this concept. It's called *"Influence: The Psychology of Persuasion"* by Robert Cialdini.

In this landmark book, Cialdini talks about a phenomenon or a rule that he calls "reciprocation." Essentially, it says that when people do a good deed, there is a need in most people to repay that person in kind. I won't go into details. Buy his book for all that. I will say that when you handle a complaint effectively, the average customer will feel a sense of obligation to reciprocate in some manner. This means that if you ask for a referral or suggest a cross-sell or whatever, there is a greater tendency for that person to respond in some positive manner.

Knowing all this going into the complaint makes the concept of converting that complaint to a sale much easier.

Two Steps For Turning Anger to Profit

The trick to turning anger to profit is having good people who know how to manage the complaint. There are two major steps to converting an unhappy customer into a purchaser. The first step is to understand why people complain. Once this it is clear, the trained rep can solve the problem by following a Three-Step process. The second step is to know when and how to apply the add-on sell.

Step 1: Understand Why People Complain

TARP has more or less written the book on customer service and, in particular, dealing with angry customers. So let's pick their collective brains for a moment longer. TARP revealed that there are three causes for customer dissatisfaction:

> *Employee based.* Roughly 20% of complaints are a direct result of poor or inadequate service provided by an employee. For example, the customer may have been given wrong or inaccurate information, or the customer may have encountered a rude employee.

> *Company based.* TARP estimates that about 30% of dissatisfaction is due to the fact that the product or service does not meet their expectations. This can cover a whole range of issues. Sometimes, it's due to overpromising in the marketing. Sometimes, it's due to failures in the system: billing errors, failure to deliver on time, etc.

> *Customer based.* About 50% of all customer complaints are a direct result of the customers themselves. Many have incorrect expectations. Others misuse the product and still others are incompetent (like me with a Palm Pilot). There is a whole host of reasons.

Okay, so what have we learned from an add-on selling point of view? Simply this: you need to be able to understand what caused the complaint before you can attempt to fix it.

Dealing with Angry Customers. There have been truckloads of books written about dealing with angry customers, not to mention seminars and workshops. These are invaluable resources and if you are in a position where angry customers are more the norm rather than the exception, then you should invest the time and money. However, to get you started, there are three simple steps to managing the anger.

A. Let them purge. Angry customers don't usually hide their dissatisfaction. They are big and bold about it. The first step is to let customers purge themselves of their anger and frustration. They are calling because something is wrong, in their minds, with you, your company, or your product. Many believe that no one really cares about their problems, so they vent as quickly as possible to demonstrate their resolve. This is their "day in court" so they feel the need to plead their cause.

Let them.

Simply sit back, shut up and listen. Take notes as you go. Give the customer calm, verbal clues that reveal you are listening and concerned. Little phrases like "I see" and "go on" will go a long way in helping mollify the customer.

The trick at this stage is to be objective and not take the remarks personally. The biggest, single mistake you can make is to feel the attack is personal. Once you have crossed that line, defensive barriers arise. Some reps get highly defensive and other will go on the offensive. Neither strategy works. So, just listen and do not react defensively.

B. Take control. The next step is to take control. *When* you take control is the key. Studies show that an individual cannot maintain angry outbursts for more than two minutes before they have to take a breath and regroup. This can be an eternity if you are on the receiving end, but two minutes is the maximum, and that's for the VERY angry customer.

At any rate, at some point, you'll recognize that the customer has vented himself for the moment and may be regrouping for another verbal volley. You'll recognize this by a distinctive pause in their dissertation.

That's the moment you take control

You take control by empathizing. You start by saying this;

"Mr. Edgerton, I understand…"

Use the customer's name. Use his SURNAME. It is more formal and respectful. You should know by now that using the name gets the person's attention. Make sure your voice is calm. Try to keep it an octave or two lower. Lower voices have a calming and more authoritative effect on the listener.

Then say,

"I want to help. Let me ask you some questions. First, when did this occur…"

Note the words here and how they work to take control. Telling the customer that you want to help is vital. It becomes a lifeline for them. "At last!" they say, "Someone who wants to help me."

Telling the customer you want to ask questions shows you are taking control. They'll recognize that. Of course, the questioning helps you clarify, but equally important, it helps move the customer from an emotional tangent to a more rationale tangent. It forces them to calm down. Subjectivity is replaced with objectivity.

Finally, move quickly and without pause into your first question. Remember, it is quite likely that the customer has paused to catch his or her breath before launching into another tirade. Don't give them the chance. Start off with two or three CLOSE ended questions. Avoid the open-ended questions at this early stage because the customer can use the opening to start afresh. The short answer question forces them to give details and reinforces the fact that you are taking control.

C. Analyze and Provide a Solution. The final step is to analyze the situation. If your questioning is effective, you'll be able to determine if the problem is with an employee, the company, or if it is customer based. The ultimate solution that you provide will depend a great deal on the cause of the problem and on the power and authority that you have been given. Some reps have the power to make decisions while others need to pass the issue on to a higher authority like a supervisor or a manager.

In your analysis of the situation, you are trying to determine if there is something specifically that can solve the problem. Often, it's a simply matter of educating the customer (remember that 50% of the time, the customers cause their own problems). Computer and software customer service reps are well aware of this. Customers become their own worst enemies by failing to follow simple procedures.

Step 2 to Turning Anger Into Profit:
Provide the Add-on Sell
Remember Cialdini's rule of reciprocation? If you solve a problem to the customer's satisfaction, a feeling of good will is created. Many customers feel either the conscious or subconscious desire to reciprocate in some way, shape or form. What this really means is they are open to listening to any special offer you have. It doesn't necessarily mean they will buy, but they are open to the suggestion.

Knowing this is powerful stuff. It should give you a psychological advantage. Or, at the very least, it should minimize any fear you might have in providing the add-on offer.

3-Step Process for Add-On Selling
On a Complaint

Step 1: Bridge to the Add-On

After you have handled the customer's complaint and you feel it has been managed satisfactorily, bridge to the add-on. Remember, the customer is basking in the glow of satisfaction. He will be receptive to listening to you. You can use the same techniques that have been offered in other chapters. For example,

> **"Ms. Sopa, I am glad we were able to straighten out the problem with the billing. While I have you…"**

> **"I am glad that the software glitch has been fixed. Mr. Bothwell, while I still have you, there's something I'd like to suggest…"**

> **"Steve, again, my apologies for the mix up on the shipping. That will be taken care of this morning. Steve, before we go, I have an idea that I would like to share with you…"**

A few tips:

Note that the customer names have been used. You might recall that when you use the customer names, they tend to focus and listen closely to the next 8-10 words.

As well, in the first example, the rep references the fact that the problem was solved. This is a superb technique and strongly recommended. By gently reminding the customer that the problem was solved you create the "reciprocating" effect mentioned by Cialdini.

Step 2: Present Your Add-On and its Benefit

As mentioned earlier, you can present virtually any add-on because the customer will be receptive. The two biggest add-on opportunities however, tend to be a cross-sell or an up-sell/upgrade. There are two approaches you can take:

Present a Product that Solves the Problem. Very often in your analysis phase of handling the complaint, you will discover that the customer's problem can be fixed with the purchase of another product or an upgrade. For example, at Komputer Korner, a computer retail store, complaints about computer crashes are a dime a dozen. A little analysis shows that shortly after they bought their computer they (or their kids) begin to load games like "Age of Empires" and "Dominion Wars", plus a whole host of other software. The end result is a computer without enough RAM...or so I am told.

The "up-sell" is simple enough: more memory. Here's what might be said:

> **"Mr. Cardy, I'm glad that I was able to help identify the problem. While I have you, I would like to recommend that you increase the amount of RAM memory in your computer. What this will do is allow you to run various applications faster and without the crashes. Of course, what this will really do is save you a ton of frustration, not to mention, the loss of any important documents."**

At Black and Decker, complaints will often be received about products like battery operated screwdrivers. Customers complain that the screwdriver does not have enough charge. Through questioning, it is often learned that the customer is trying to use the tool to drive two-and-one-half inch screws through dry wall and wood. The screw driver was not designed for industrial use, but

rather for home use. The Black and Decker rep solves the
problem with this recommendation:

> **"Mr. Ramsay, as I have indicated, the
> battery operated screwdriver is designed for
> casual use around the home. I have an idea
> however, that might help. If you are
> planning to do more heavy labor in your
> basement, I'd like to recommend our variable
> speed drill. It comes with two powerful,
> rechargeable batteries plus attachments that
> can handle any type of screw. You can use
> the electrical screwdriver for small jobs be-
> cause it is handy, and use the variable speed
> drill for the more labor-intensive jobs. In the
> end, what this will do is save you time and of
> course, frustration."**

Here are some simple rules to follow when presenting a
product that solves a problem.

- First, present the offer. Make it clear what it is
  you're recommending.

- Second, provide a clear and if necessary, in depth
  explanation of what the offer will do. The biggest,
  single mistake made by sales and customer service
  reps alike is assuming that the client understands
  your products as well as you. They don't. I don't.
  What is obvious to you is not obvious to most of
  your customers. So be prepared and have a clear,
  concise explanation.

- Third, make your benefit clear. If the customer
  was experiencing frustration, explain how the
  product will eliminate it.

Present an Unrelated Product. The product that you offer does not necessarily have to solve a problem. TARP has shown that the tendency to buy ANY related product is strong.

Polaroid, the camera and film company, learned this. For example, they discovered that professional photographers who had their problems solved were very receptive to cross-sells such as photo enlargers and enhancers. What is interesting is that these products are not inexpensive. A sizeable investment was required. But again, the power of satisfaction is so strong that it creates a motivation to buy.

If this is true, and it is, then asking for a referral or qualifying a lead for a higher ticket item is a simple extension.

Step 4: Close

You must have closure. I won't flog this one to death. Present the price and ask for the sale. The customer needs this step in order to take action.

> **"An additional 64Mgs of RAM is just $60.00 installed. How does that sound?"**

> **"The variable speed drills with the batteries and attachments, including a recharger is only $129.00. Would you like to place that order?"**

Summary

Complaints can be profitable. But because so much emotion is often accompanied with a complaint, any thought of add-on selling would typically be ignored. Don't let the opportunity pass you by. Learn to listen to the problem. Seek to find a solution. Then, if you do, satisfy the customer, then leverage the moment and present your add-on.

Chapter 10

Gathering Market Intelligence

Just suppose for a minute or two that you could have an endless stream of information that told you what your customers liked or disliked about your company? Suppose you could discover what your competition was offering and why prospects were buying from them? And since we're still supposing, suppose there was a way to tap into marketplace trends early? And suppose you could use this information to spin on a dime and adjust your approach overnight? What would that do for you and your company?

That's what this chapter is about.

This chapter is about gathering market intelligence from your customer and prospects. It's about gathering information with each and every call. It's about gauging your marketplace and at virtually no cost. It's about a way to leverage the moment.

What Is "Market Intelligence?"
Market intelligence. Talk about a sexy phrases!

It is not really complex. What market intelligence really means is the gathering of information from your clients and prospects so that you can analyze your marketplace, your customers, your competitors, and your products and services.

Don't mistake market intelligence gathering for "market research." Market research implies large surveys, focus groups, statistical analysis and regression, and all that other hocus pocus to help understand the workings of your marketplace.

Market intelligence is a poor man's version of market research. It is not nearly so stuffy, much less formal and far easier to collect and analyze. Admittedly, it does not have the same scientific bend as formal market research, but by asking your clients/prospects a few key questions on incoming and outgoing calls, you can gain hundreds, if not thousands of impressions about any topic you choose.

The sheer numbers can give you an accurate, if not statistically valid, picture of your marketplace from which you can make any number of strategic and tactical decisions.

What's Your ROI For Market Intelligence?
Who's to say, really?

Machiavelli, the famed Florentine who wrote the book, *The Prince* commented, "information is power."

Bull.

Information is *not* power. It is what you **do** with the information that creates the power. If you gather data and ignore it, your ROI is negative. If you gather data, analyze it and respond accordingly, your ROI can be significant.

We'll see some examples in a moment.

Strategically, armed with insights on customers, prospects, competitors, market trends and the like, the savvy sales/marketing/customer service executive has the potential to:

- adjust, alter, or even cancel strategies,

- reposition its product,

- change a marketing message,

- adjust a script used by reps,

- assess an offer,

- redefine its target market, or,

- respond to competitive threats.

The list goes on.

Three Applications
Gathering market intelligence is really a broad term that can cover any number of topics. Here are three specific examples where it applies:

1. Target Market Intelligence
One of the most powerful and effective applications of gathering market intelligence is using a call to learn more about your target market: about those who use your product/service or those who have the potential to use your product/service.

Far too many businesses have a broad, in not vague, idea of exactly who buys their products and services, what motivates them to take action and what they really want. If your company is small-to-medium-sized, take a close look at this application. Smaller companies typically don't have the budget and time to hire market research firms to provide them with critical data. Here is a cost effective way to learn more about what your target markets think and want.

Here's a good example. A while ago, a small insurance firm offered pet insurance to cat and dog owners. Yes, you read that correctly. Bizarre as it sounds, the insurance provided sickness, injury and death coverage for Spot and Fluffy. For pet owners it can be a big thing. In fact, over 70% of pet owners see their cat or dog as one of the family.

In any event, the target market was broadly defined as "upper income" (i.e., those with enough disposable income to invest in a pet policy). The main selling message was the money one would save when given the veterinarian's bill. While the company sold policies, pet owners did not necessarily beat a path to the door.

To get a better grip on who was buying and why, the company began to ask a few simple questions at the end of every incoming and outgoing call to both prospects and clients. For example, the company would ask who was the primary care giver of the pet, what was motivating them to call about insurance, and a brief profile on their lifestyle.

Within a couple of weeks and armed with hundreds of mini-interviews, the target was more precisely defined as a female, mid thirties in age, post secondary education, full or part-time job, children and the primary care giver to the pet. But here's the clincher: the primary motivator for buying insurance was *not* saving money. The primary motivator was emotional. The motivator was based on the pain/fear of the pet suffering or dying because they could not afford the cost of treatment. It was a subtle but hugely significant motivator. *Saving* money was not the issue; issue; the pet's well-being and care was the issue. Saving money was not nearly as important as having the ability to pay for treatments that could save the pet from suffering.

As a result, of this new target market focus, advertising and promotional campaigns were changed. They appealed to the female caregiver and they appealed to the heart-string buying motive. Sure, saving money was still part of the message. You can't ignore that element. But the real emphasis was on the health of the pet and, more discreetly, the implications if the pet was gone. Ultimately, it allowed the company to more precisely identifying the best print media for it to advertise. This meant the advertising budget was used more effectively. Brochures were changed to reflect families and their pets; close ups where taken of women and their cat or dog. That's good marketing. Bottom line? Significantly better response and significantly better close ratio.

2. Competitive Market Intelligence
A while ago, I was working with buystream.com, a company that sells software for web designers. A huge push was on to gather information about competitive products. The inside reps did what sales reps have been doing for decades: they'd call the competitors and request that literature be sent to them. Typically, a home address was provided.

There is nothing particularly wrong about this approach. It has been a time-honored strategy. Heck, I use this approach myself.

But, buystream.com and yours truly must be aware of two key points. First, the information we collect via competitor literature is the information that they share with the world. It is written and positioned to heighten the value of their product. It was written to sell. In short, competitive literature is grossly biased…and misleading.

This leads to the second point. Buystream.com and yours truly must be careful not to ignore the best source of information, i.e., those businesses that purchase competitive products. It is vital to understand why others bought competitive product. What motivated them to buy? Was it price? Was it an issue of trust? Was it the product? And so on.

You would be stunned at what prospect and customers will tell you about your competitors–if you ask.

What makes their statements so powerful is that they are the users of the competitive products. They will tell you why THEY bought the product; what their perception of your competitor is. When you think about it, is doesn't really matter what your competitor promises, it is what your target market believes or perceives to be true.

Here's a perfect example. Let's go re-visit Grand and Toy, the office supply and products company. The chain was being hit heavily by the "big box" superstores. Overall, price was perceived to the key reason why customers where drifting off to the superstores. But just to be sure, questions were added to outbound calls made to small and medium sized business customers to get an idea about why they were purchasing from the larger stores.

Price rose its head from time-to-time but a great many stores discovered that access to their storefront was a critical issue. For the most part, Grand and Toy has located their stores in malls which made access to parking a little more difficult, if only because the customer had to park the vehicle some distance from the store and thread his way through the mall. Business customers did not find this terribly convenient. While Grand and Toy offered free delivery, it quickly became obvious that the average small business was totally unaware of this service.

The answer?

Advise the customer. Educate them that they don't have to drive to a mall, park and jockey their way through three levels of the mall to get to the store. Make it a part of their message. Don't wait for the objection. Consequently, their rep who made outbound calls to existing clients began to inform customers that delivery was free, and in most cases, could be provided the same day if not the next. The result was phenomenal.

But consider the alternative. If price was assumed to be the most important issue, Grand and Toy would have responded with pricing strategies that may or may not have worked. Certainly, it would have cut into their margin. It's a issue of diagnosis. If your diagnosis is incorrect, things won't improve. That can cost time, money and effort.

3. Product/Service Intelligence

The final application is product intelligence. If you want to find out more about what your product or service does (or can do) for your customers, ask them.

Steve Jobs, the founder and chairman of Apple Computers, once commented that his best research and development team was not Apple's hired staff of gurus, whiz kids and geeks but rather users (customers) of Apple products. The users would tinker with the computer and the software and discover or suggest all sorts of applications that Apple never imagined. Their discoveries and recommendations are routinely incorporated with each and every new Apple product.

Perhaps one the best told examples of using customers as a sounding board for product intelligence is General Electric. The famed GE Call Center takes thousands of calls from customers answering a myriad of questions concerning dozens of products. At some point, someone within GE began to recognize that these calls were a potential source of market research.

Here is a timeless example. GE manufactured dryers that were equipped with a loud automatic buzzer that advised the user that a cycle was complete. It was an excellent feature for most, but not all users. In particular, mothers with newborn babies found that the buzzer would wake up their child with its piercing alarm. (Speaking from personal experience, waking up a napping baby is not a good thing!)

Consumers told GE how much they liked the dryer but suggested that GE add an on/off switch. This they did. And

the rest, as they say, is history. The real point is this: the users of your products can tell you how to make your product better, more effective, more user-friendly…
…whatever.

The same holds true in service related fields. Myers Chevy Olds is a General Motors car dealership in Nepean, Ontario. Myers has an almost fanatical approach to assessing customer satisfaction. Loryanne Schultz, the Director of Marketing and Customer Communications constantly uses their call center to gauge customer opinions. They will call a new car owner to assess their experience with the sale representative who sold them the car. They will call car owners who recently had their car serviced to determine the level of satisfaction with everything from the repairs, to the service advisor…you name it.

Myers has used the information to adjust its staff and its service. For instance, their service bays have been completely revamped to making getting in and out of service faster and hassle free. One set of doors in the service department handles oil, lube and filter customers; another set handles those clients who have appointments for more major concerns.

The result? Faster service, less wait, greater customer satisfaction, return customers, referrals, repeat buys. Not bad, eh?

The Four-Step Process for Gathering Intelligence
Talk about your "no brainer." Gathering market intelligence is fast and easy.

Step 1: Handle the Initial Request, Inquiry, Order, Complaint, etc.

This add-on rule does not change. It never does. Handle the customer's or prospect's initial request before you do anything else. You must provide service first before requesting the information. Enough said about that.

Step 2: Bridge to the Request

The rule doesn't change here either. Why would it? You need to advise the customer that here is a subtle shift in the conversation. You need to prepare them and ask if it is okay to ask some questions. Here are some examples.

> **"Mr. Ferrenti, while I have you, I wonder if I might take thirty seconds of your time and ask you some questions regarding the service on your Trail Blazer?"**

> **"Pat, could I trouble you for one more minute of your time and ask you four quick questions?"**

> **"Mr. Mews, could I borrow another twenty or thirty seconds of your time and ask you a few questions?"**

Three Bridging Tips

Note that each of these bridging statements has two critical elements that you should incorporate. Let's look at each because, not only do they increase the receptivity of the client, they help ensure a better quality answer.

Be Humble. The first is the "humble" approach. Your words and your tone must be humble. Humble does not mean meek and mild. It means respectful.

Using words like "I wonder" or "Could I trouble you?" or "Could I borrow…?" trigger a positive response from clients. Trust me. These words suggest you are asking a "favor" and clients tend to have more time and patience when it is so positioned. They open up. These phrases are also non-threatening to the client. They are not pressure words. Defensive barriers typically drop.

Give a Timeframe. My experience with dozens of marketing intelligence gathering programs has shown that putting a specific time limit on the request increases receptivity. Vague requests like "Could I take a few minutes…?" turns off many people. Most people perceive "a few minutes," as many, many minutes. They become suspect and impatient. They don't want to be surveyed for "ten minutes". It was not part of the bargain. Giving them some sort of time perspective will help them determine if they will or will not comply.

Keep the timeframe short. Let's carry this to its logical conclusion. To get quality information, keep it short. No more than a minute or two. No more.

I have seen companies who unintentionally abuse the moment by trying to cram as many questions as possible into the call. Not only does the client get annoyed, the information provided becomes diluted and inaccurate as the client tries to hurry the conversation.

REMEMBER: This is market intelligence, not market research. If you want detailed information, you should be conducting a formal study. Market intelligence implies short and fast bits of information. This means you have to really think about what it is you want to learn and craft three or four questions to meet your objective.

Step 3: Present the Reason and the Benefit
WARNING! This is important:

The most common mistake is to NOT explain to your client the reason and the benefit for taking the time to respond to your questions. Here's why. Once the customer understands your request, they tend to give you better information. Quality is what you are after. The higher the quality of information, the better you are able to use it.

One of the biggest concerns when gathering market intelligence is information that is given "off the cuff" and, as mentioned, diluted because the client is impatient or unsure of why you want it. False or inaccurate information can and will lead to mediocre or poor results. In some cases, it could be disastrous. False or diluted information is a waste of your client's time and a waste of your time.

Oh yeah, one more thing. If the customer finds the exercise a waste of time, the NEXT time you want to gather intelligence he or she will be considerably less receptive.

Presenting the reason and benefit need not be complex. Here are some examples.

> **"Mr. Ferrenti, while I have you, I wonder if I might take thirty seconds of your time and ask you some questions regarding the service on your Trail Blazer? We are always assessing our job functions to look for ways that we might improve or enhance service. How does that sound?"**

The reason/benefit is simple. It is implied that an improvement of service will be beneficial for the client.

> **"Pat, could I trouble you for one more minute of your time and ask you four quick questions? We are attempting to better understand our client base so that we can de-**

126

velop new products to meet the changing needs of pet owners. Do you have a moment?"

"Mr. Mews, could I borrow another twenty or thirty seconds of your time and ask you a few questions? Our goal is to better understand how customers like yourself are using our software so that we can enhance features to make the software more versatile and user friendly. Okay?"

Here are a few tips.

You may have seen this tip in other chapters and might be tired of seeing it. But, get used to it. After you have made your request and presented the benefits, do this:

SHUT UP!

I do not agree with the strategy of barreling forward and launching into the questions before the customers has agreed to your request. There are those who might argue this point but again, I go to the issue of quality. If the client agrees, he or she is more likely to provide better information.

So, what next?

One of three things will happen after you make your request:

1. The client says yes. If they say yes, thank them and move quickly into the questioning phase. Don't fumble about and waste anymore time.

2. The client says no. If they reply no, simply reply "I understand." Go on to thank the customer for their initial request, order or whatever and then terminate the call.

DO NOT treat the no as an objection that you must overcome. Remember the add-on is an add-on. It's a bonus if they agree. If they do not agree, do not belabor the point. It will only annoy them. Big time. If they are not receptive, don't make a big deal out of it.

3. The client has a question. Occasionally you will encounter clients who want to know what kind of information and/or precisely why you are gathering data. I mention this because there is a growing concern among many consumers that there is too much information floating around out there about personal issues.

Responses like "Well, I'm not really sure," or "They just told me to ask," or "We're just sort of collecting stuff," simply does not cut the mustard for the average customer.

You must do two things here. First, anticipate the type of questions you will encounter. Preparation is the key. Sit down as a group and brainstorm. No question is ridiculous. If you can think of it, so can you customer.

Second, use a job aid to help you respond. (See: Chapter 18: "Add-on Selling Job Aids"). An "objections chart" is a tool where you can record your responses to an objection. It makes your job easier and faster. When you hear an objection, you can glance at the chart and have a reply already formulated.

Step 4: Close
By close, I am referring here to the end of the call, after you have gathered the market intelligence.

I have some tips for effective questioning coming up, but first let me say that when you have completed the questions, simply thank the customer and terminate the call. They are ready to hang up so don't prolong the issue.

Five Vital Tips On Questioning
Here are some key points when crafting your questions Pay close attention to them!

1. The Number of Questions is Important
Excuse me if I flog this horse to death. It's worth the time and space. Customers and prospects have an internal tolerance level. Your questions were not part of the original call so they will answer them.

Speaking of tolerance, here's an interesting insight. Based on experience, the average client will answer four questions with relative comfort and tolerance. Beyond that, intolerance sets in and the quality of information received will become diluted.

So, your questions should be limited to a maximum of four.

2. The Types of Questions are Critical
If you've taken any sort of communications or selling course you will know that there are two types of questions you can ask: open and closed.

Open-ended questions solicit ideas, opinions, and concepts because they get the client to open up. Questions that begin with "Describe, tell, explain, why, etc." invite elaboration. Close-ended questions gather precise data, facts, details. They don't invite the client to expand. They are used to help clarify, verify and confirm.

But, while each has their charms, they also have their demons. You need to be aware of these demons before you implement your questioning.

Open-Ended Demons. The open-ended question elicits longer and, often, more complex responses from your client. The problem is fourfold. First, the longer the response means the more time the rep spends on the telephone. This can impact productivity and answer rates.

Secondly, and perhaps more importantly, is the fact that the information provided by the customer is hard to collect. In other words, someone has to record the information on paper or into the computer. Rarely can a rep write or type as fast as someone speaks. Of course, what this really means is that it is sometimes hard to catch everything that is provided and record it accurately.

The third little demon is that open-ended questions solicit information that is interpretive. The rep is forced to synthesize what they hear and interpret the meaning. That can be dangerous because it relies on the rep's ability to consistently understand the client's complex thoughts. Sounds confusing and virtually impossible? Yep.

The fourth and final demon is that open-ended questions lead to all sorts of forks in the road. In other words, they are hard to control because the customer follows trains of thought that are important to him or her.

Gee, does that mean we avoid open-ended question completely?

No.

But, you must make sure that your question is clear so that the customer stays focused. Focus is the key. The other thing is you should rarely ask more than a couple of open-ended questions. Why? Because they take time and with time, client tolerance is reduced.

Closed-Ended Demons. Close-ended questions are not without their demons too. But, there really is only two to deal with.

The first demon is that closed-ended questions gather short, precise, factual data. They do not get into interpretative analysis. For instance, here's a closed-ended question that can be misleading.

> *"What is more important to you: value or price?"*

The question seems clear enough and it is closed-ended. The answer is either value or price. But if the customer says value, it begs the question, "What does value mean to you?" Value is a moving target with each and every consumer and business. What is value to me may be a standard expectation to you. Similarly, if the customer says price is important, it does not necessarily mean that he or she is looking for the lowest possible price.

Here again, you have think about your questions carefully. Look at them from all angles. For example, the question above might be better phrased with an open-ended question such as,

> **"Mr. Ford, what factors impact how you buy?"**

Or you might use a scale system:

> **"Ms. Donaldson, on a scale of one to five, with five being the highest and one the lowest, how would you rate the following in your decision, buying process: price, delivery, service, selection?"**

Even this approach has its potential flaws. And that's why it is important to understand that what information you do gather is considered "market intelligence" rather than market research.

131

The second little demon is that too many consecutive, close-ended questions can sound like an interrogation. The customer or the prospect can feel like they are being grilled because there is little dialogue. The moment they feel like this, the quality plummets.

3. Managing the Questioning Process is Critical

To ensure that the customer does not feel like they are being grilled by "Dragnet's" Sergeant Joe Friday, you can manage the question process quite simply.

At the end of every two questions, interject a dose of humanity. By that I mean soften the process by adding a little phrase or two like,

> **"...okay, we've only got two more questions..."**

> **"...that's a good point...just one more question..."**

> **"...this is really good information, Mr. Craig. We're almost done..."**

These little phrases extent the tolerance level and reduce the feeling that the questions are an interrogation.

4. Record the Data

You will need some way to capture and record the information. You can record the data on paper or your computer, or, if you're real ambitious, on tape. The pros and cons of these options are fairly obvious and I won't beat them to death.

5. DO Something With It

Let's go back to Machiavelli. Information is not power, only potential power. Gathering the information is one thing. Analyzing it and doing something with it, is another. Someone has to look at the data. At the end of the day, if you don't respond to the market intelligence, your efforts were wasted. Better to cross-sell, up-sell or gather a referral than to waste the time.

Summary

Market intelligence can be a great way to get a competitive edge in your business. By adding a few questions onto every call you make or take, you can get an instant feel for what is happening in the marketplace. This can be powerful stuff, so use it.

One last reminder, again, market intelligence is not market research.

Chapter 11

Getting a Referral

(and never having to cold call again)

If you're in sales, this is a MUST READ chapter.

If part of your job requires you to make cold calls, then you will know how frosty the response can sometimes be. Suppose you could thaw that cold call? Suppose you could speed up the sales cycle and get more sales and less rejection? Would that make your sales life a little easier?

The way to warm up the cold call is by using a referral. And that's precisely what this chapter is all about. Plainly put, we'll look at how to get a referral from your customers and prospects, whether they buy from you or not. There are a couple of great examples in the chapter, including the "Referral Queen", Elizabeth Fisher, who closes about 100% of the referrals she gets.

We'll also talk about a technique called "Referencing". It is way of asking for the client to service as a testimonial or a reference for any future prospects. Not many reps do this and it's a crying shame. Pay heed to this one.

All About Referrals

Getting a referral is the practice of obtaining a name of a potential prospect from an existing customer or prospect. It's that simple.

So why do it? Here's a startling sales reality. Most sales reps are not as successful as they can possibly be, NOT because they can't sell or because they have nothing good to sell, but rather because they do not have enough access to buyers. Finding the right buyer is tough. Getting the buyer to make a purchase decision is even tougher.

Can you blame 'em? Put yourself in the buyers' shoes. Buyers are leery about purchasing from people and companies that they don't know well. In today's market, and thanks in large part to the telephone, buyers are inundated with dozens of calls. While this means they have a choice from whom to buy, it also means they have the confusion and hassle of determining whom to trust. Therein lies the issue. Trust.

Building trust takes time. Typically, trust is built through a series of steps, all of which takes time and effort. In sales, we have learned to accept this. But it doesn't necessarily have to take as much time and effort as it normally does.

Enter the referral. With a good referral, the buyer tends to listen more closely and is far more receptive to you. Assuming they have an affinity with the person who referred them, the buyer is more apt to take the chance. Buyers can call the person who referred them and get the skinny on you and you're your company.

So, put succinctly, the referrals reduce the time it takes to sell and increase the closing rate because there is an element of trust.

Get this: some studies reveal that typical cold-calling will eventually net a 10% close rate. Not great. Compare this with referral calling that can garner anywhere from 25% - 80% close rates!

And if that isn't enough, a referral comes with little or no cost whatsoever. You get the referral at the end of a call. It takes perhaps a minute of your time.

Three Reasons Why We Don't Ask For Referrals

The evidence is overwhelming. Referrals work. Yet despite all this, sales reps tend to ignore or avoid the process of getting referrals. There are three reasons for this.

1. Fear of Rejection

Scratch the surface deep enough and you will find that many sales reps fear the referral process. They don't want to be seen as impolite, aggressive, intrusive and pushy. They worry that they'll somehow offend their client. Ultimately, they fear that they will be rejected if they attempt the referral.

Look, this is an emotional, not a logical issue. As noted author and publisher, Art Sobczak, puts it, common sense tells us that people who already enjoy the benefits of what you provide are the most likely candidates to wish the same for their friends, peers, and associates. If you have done a bang-up job servicing or selling a customer, they are pleased and happy with the benefits they are deriving. This means they are positive and receptive to you. Asking for a referral is not a nasty or manipulative tactic.

In fact, Sobczak quotes Ted Kurtz, a psychoanalyst and consultant in Cold Spring Harbor, New York, as saying that people give referrals because:

- They like the *prestige* of being asked. Many see it as compliment. Call it a sense of power, if you like.

- They like "being in the know." They see themselves as being viewed as the *Consumer Reports* of products and services. They are a champion.

- They want to *help* you. You've done a good job so they want to help you out. Some people are nice that way.

- They want to help out their peers, friends, associates. They want their friends to succeed. Again, I suspect there is a "champion" mentality at work here. They've stumbled onto a good thing, they share it, and they're seen as been helpful.

I could probably add another one, though I am not an esteemed psychoanalyst. But personally, when I pass on a referral, there is a part of me that hopes their favor will be returned some day. I hope that maybe my friend, peer or associate will remember what I did and when an opportunity arises, he or she will reciprocate.

So, the point is, get rid of this wimpy rejection thing. For goodness sakes, the worst anyone will say to you is "no".

That's it.

They will not viciously attack you. This, I promise.

2. They Tried it and it Didn't Work
The second reason that sales reps don't ask for referrals is that they tried it and it didn't work. Translated, what this really means is that they tried it once or twice and did not get a referral, so they got discouraged and gave up. This is sort of like the rejection thing above, but at least they gave it a try.

3. They Don't Know How
The third reason is that reps don't know how to effectively ask for a referral. Consequently, some never bother to ask simply because they don't know what to do or say. Chances are, that the reps who tried it and found "it didn't work" ,didn't to know to ask for a referral.

The Four-Step Process for Asking for Referrals
Asking for a referral is not the least bit difficult and it can follow the same process that's been outlined in the previous chapters.

Step 1: Handle the Initial Order or Request
Don't forget, the referral is an add-on sale. You must handle the initial task at hand. I know this is probably obvious by now but in order for you to get a referral, the client must be happy or satisfied with his or her experience. Satisfaction will mean the client is more receptive to helping you out. This is why everything, absolute everything you do from the beginning of a call or a visit to the end, must be done thoroughly and professionally. I have said it before: PLEASE SWEAT THE SMALL STUFF.

Step 2: Bridge to the Add-On
Here again, the same bridges that can be used for other applications apply here:

> **"…Dave, while I have you…"**

> **"…Debbie, if I could just take another minute…"**

> **"…Mr. Worman, one more thing…"**

We do this because the bridge alerts your client that something else is coming up. It gets their attention and focus. Remember to use the client's name because it gets him or her to listen more closely to your next phrase.

Step 3: Present the Request For a Referral and Benefit
Okay: there is a right way and a not-so-right way to ask for referrals.

The Not-So-Right Way. The not-so-right way looks something like this.

> *"Jean-Pierre, do you know anybody who might use our products?"*
>
> *"Eleanor, can you give me a couple of names of people who might be interested in my services?*

On the surface these phrases seem okay…and to be technical…they are "okay". It does work. What these phrases lack is a benefit statement. It is important that you remind the client of the benefit (the savings, the pleasure, the fun…whatever) they have derived.

However, there is one drawback. These phrases make it easy to say "no".

The Right Way. The right way, or should I say, the more *effective* way to ask for a referral looks like this.

> **"Jean-Pierre, thank you for your order. Listen, Jean-Pierre, while I have you…who do you know who has the same requirements (for cost savings, speedy delivery, technical support…) that I could contact and review what we might be able to do for them?"**

Not much of a difference between this phrase and the two cited above. However, the use of the phrase "Who do you know who…?" has shown to be very effective at eliciting a referral. You see, with a phrase like this, it is virtually impossible for your client to say "no".   The question doesn't invite it. The question invites thought and introspection.

Sure, it's subtle. But sales is very often a subtle art. Don't believe me? Test them. Test them both and see what works better. Let me know how you do. But whatever you do, ask for a referral.

The Referral Queen

Elizabeth Fisher of Omni Partners has been dubbed the "Referral Queen" by those with whom she works. Omni Partners is an executive recruitment firm where the stakes are high and the market is very competitive. To succeed, you need to have an "in" and Fisher's "in" is referrals. Elizabeth asks for a referral from clients and prospects alike regardless of the circumstances. At the end of the day, she might only garner a small handful of referrals, but what is more significant is that she will close virtually 100% of the referrals she gets!

We'll look at her straightforward technique with clients and prospects.

Clients. Of course, dealing with a satisfied client is the most ideal situation. So, when the opportunity arises, Elizabeth will say something like,

> **"Jim, who do you know who might benefit from my services?"**

(Remember Elizabeth is with a recruiting firm. Chances Are, she has just placed an executive who has moved on to a bigger and/better job. The benefits from her services are evident.)

The client will do one of two things:

- the client gives Elizabeth a referral and bang, she's off, or,

- the client does not offer a name.

But here's where Fisher has earned her title as the Referral Queen. If the client does not have a referral name, she prompts them a bit further to jog their memory. She starts internally. For example,

> **"Is there someone in another division or a department that might benefit from my services?"**

What Fisher has learned is a name does not always spring to mind. Not so much because of internal resistance but rather because she has caught the client a bit off guard. Prompting keeps the discussion open and, if you like, casts the net wider. If the internal prompt doesn't work, Elizabeth will dig deeper. Call this the "external prompt."

> **"Jim you're highly involved in the industry. Is there anyone you know in the industry that might be interested in the services I provide?"**

Again, the idea here is for the client to think on a larger scale. It is that sort of tenacity that pays dividends.

Prospects. While clients are typically your best source for referrals, prospects can sometimes offer up a name or two. Elizabeth will cold-call prospects. Sometimes, of course, the call does not pan out, but that does not deter her. For example,

> **"Marianna, thank you for your time. It looks like there is not a fit at this moment but I will contact you in a month or so to determine if your needs have changed. In the meantime, while I have you, who do you know who might benefit from my services?"**

Elizabeth will also go through the same prompts, moving internally to externally. Obviously, Fisher knows her business. In executive recruitment, executives talk to their friends and peers. They put out feelers to see what's going on in the market; to determine their worth or value. Armed with this knowledge, Fisher knows a polite, courteous prompt can generate an excellent lead.

It is worth mentioning again because the results are stunning. In any given day, Elizabeth might generate only one or two referrals. But they are good. At last count, her rate was about 100%. It can't get any better than that.

The Internal Referral. Elizabeth used it. All smart reps use it. It's called the internal referral.

The internal referral is used to find referrals within your client's own business. This is a great way to get strong referrals in larger companies. The reason why it works is that the when you call the referral, they have an internal source who can vouch for you and your products. The "organizational leap of faith" is as easy as a hop, skip and a jump.

Vernon Computer Rentals rents computers to businesses rather than selling or leasing them. They have carved themselves a good little niche with those companies who don't want to be tied to technology, which in three to six months will be obsolete. Vernon uses the internal referral because they typically deal with large companies with multiple departments.

For example, if Vernon converts a department to rentals in, say, Nortel, the reps will ask:

**"Barry, are you aware of any other depart-
ments or labs who might be restructuring
their computers?"**

Inevitably, they catch wind of a department or two. Simple stuff. Good stuff.

The Reference. The reference is a slightly different version of the referral. The reference is where you ask the client if he or she can be used as a reference for other prospects. In effect, you are asking the client if they will be a "talking testimonial" for you, your company, and/or your products or services. You can ask for the reference whether you have gotten a referral or not.

> **"Ms. Holt, I get the impression that our company (product/service) has done a good job for you in (state   benefit: e.g., saving money, reducing deliver times, etc.). Am I right in that assumption?"**

> **"I'm really glad to hear that. Ms. Holt, could I use you and your situation as a reference for certain prospects who might be in a similar situation?"**

The request has three components. First, it reminds the client of the benefits he or she has derived from the purchase of your product or service. Second, it confirms that satisfaction. Finally, it "closes" the client by asking for permission.

Easily nine customers out of ten will agree to this. They feel good right now. They're warmed by the benefits. Your request is so simple and so easy to grant that they rarely refuse.

Just a quick note: should you have to use the reference: Always make sure you call the customer to let him or her know that a call might come.

Summary
Referrals are an extremely effective way to generate additional revenues. Incredibly, very few reps ask for referrals. What this really means is that your clients are ripe for the picking. So pick!

Chapter 12

How to Generate and Qualify a Lead

Never forget one important point:

Your customers and prospects are usually unaware of ALL the products and services you have to offer.

The reason for this?

No one has told them, or no one has reminded them lately. This, of course, is the entire premise of "add-on selling".

Many of you will have products or services that are available to your clients, but typically they are more complex or more costly than up-sell or cross-sell products. And that's where lead generation and qualification kicks in. Every call you take or make may have the potential for a greater sale down the line. By asking a few, well-planned questions, you can determine if there is potential.

This chapter is not about "selling" a prospect. It is about determining if there is a potential sale down the line. It is about generating and qualifying a lead that can be worked by you or by someone else at a later date. In this chapter, we'll look at the rules of qualification, the Four-Step Process, and we'll conclude with some vital tips on how to ensure the entire process of lead generation is effectively managed.

Five Compelling Reasons Why You Should Do It
The overall benefits of increased sales should be enough incentive to implement the program, but there are few more considerations.

1. High Response
Asking a few questions is easy to do and more significantly, the customer/prospect has a greater propensity to respond. This is not a cold-call. A dialogue has already been established. Since the lead generation comes at the end of the call, a measure of rapport has been established. The end result is that the client usually responds positively to your prospecting.

2. High Affinity
The client has a greater chance of being a good candidate for other products and services you have to offer because an affinity has been established. An order might have already been taken or an inquiry made or even a complaint taken. The client is targeted. They know you and your products. Logically and by extension, further products or services might apply.

3. High Conversion
When you add high response with high affinity, you often get a higher conversion rate. The beauty of adding on a lead qualification to your existing contact is that you are eliminating the dreaded "cold call." Overall, that means greater success, better sales, commissions, customer satisfaction … the whole kit and kaboodle.

4. Low Cost
Not everyone looks at this factor but if you're a sales/marketing manager, it is an important considera-

tion. The cost of generating and qualifying a lead, much less converting it, can be very costly. Trade shows, direct mail, cold calls, print advertising and other promotional events can be timely and costly. Adding a few qualifying questions to the end of a call is extremely cost-effective.

5. *Great Disqualifier*
Here's a slightly different approach to the issue. Asking qualifying questions can disqualify the client. That might seem like a bit of a negative on the surface. After all, your objective is to get qualified leads, right?

Well, as I have said before "'yes'" lives in the land of "'no'". To get a qualified lead, you have to get rid of those who aren't qualified. By doing so, you save a ton of time and effort. By doing so, you work those leads that have a more legitimate chance of being converted.

Call it a philosophy. I look upon disqualification as a good thing. If I have a thirty percent lead generation rate, I know that I have to disqualify seventy percent of the those with whom I speak. For every one I disqualify, I feel I am that much closer to getting to those who are qualified. I see this as a positive. This way, I don't get discouraged.

When I hear that the prospect does not fit my criteria, I say "Great! I don't have to waste my time sending literature and making endless follow-up calls and then, ultimately, get discouraged."

When Should You Attempt to Generate a Lead… And When You Should Not
Virtually any situation lends itself to a generating a lead. Inquiries, complaints, customer service calls, and orders all lend themselves to this application.

However, I would caution against "piling on". Piling on is when you get a little too greedy about leveraging the contact. For example, you take an order and then cross-sell. That's good. But some business will pile on and attempt to generate and qualify a lead. Yes, from time to time it will work, but for the most part it annoys the client. They hadn't bargained on that. You got the cross-sell or up-sell. Don't push it. You'll see this a little further on in the chapter, but clients have a tolerance factor. They will tolerate longer call lengths and add-on selling only to a degree.

If you're going to use add-on selling to generate a lead, focus wholly on the lead generation and don't dilute it with other add-on selling applications. Lead generation often works on a campaign basis. In other words, there is a push to drive sales of a certain product or service. If so, work that campaign and work it well. Stay focused. You'll get far better results because the "tolerance factor" hasn't been pushed.

Forewarned is forearmed.

The Two Rules of Qualification

First of all, let's get something very clear here. Lead generation and qualification is the process where a prospect is questioned to determine if there is a possible need or application for a product or service you sell. It is not a sale. It is only a potential sale. It is the first step in a selling cycle.

The implication is that there will be a follow-up contact either by a you or by someone else further down the road. That follow-up call will continue the sales cycle to its logical end. The real point here is that the job is not to sell the product or the service but to move to qualify or disqualify the client for further contact.

The following are some critical rules for qualification on the add-on sell.

1. Limit Your Questions

Here's where the tolerance factor kicks in. Clients have a certain amount of "allotted" time for a call they have placed or taken. Granted, it is a nebulous kind of time-frame. No one consciously says this call will be precisely two minutes and 34 seconds or this visit 28 minutes. Someone who calls Victoria's Secret, for example, to place an order can consciously or subconsciously expect to take three-to-five minutes for the call to be placed.

When it goes beyond that point, a line is crossed. The client moves from tolerance to impatience. The quality of the conversation after the line has been crossed drops like a stone from a high building: fast and furious.

So, what does this mean to add-on selling?

This means you have to limit your questions. What's the right number? Well, studies show that when you ask questions at the end of a call or contact, the tolerance level rarely goes beyond five.

Don't ask me why? My own personal experience as a recipient of qualifying questions seems to bear it out. I lose interest and patience beyond this point. I use it as a rule of thumb and I suggest you do too.

RULE OF THUMB
No more than 5 questions!

2. Ask the Right Questions

Well, if you can only ask a maximum of five questions, then every bone in your body should tell you to maximize those questions. That means you must ask the *right* questions.

The right questions will vary from company to company and from product to product. I cannot give you the right set of questions, but I can list some general categories that seem to arise for most organizations.

Fundamental Questions – You need a question or two that determines if there is a fundamental need for the product. For example, Cybermation Inc., is a provider of work scheduling software. Before they can even hope to sell, they must know if the client has an Enterprise System. Don't worry about what this is. The point is, if the prospect does not have it, there is no chance of pursing it further.

Time Questions – Time questions are those that relate to the timeframe that a client has in mind to make a decision. By way of example, Marsh Inc., is a very large brokerage firm that will attempt to collect expiry dates for property and casualty insurance. If the expiry date is ten or twelve months away, the lead is not "hot" and will not be worked on right away. Of course, a lead that is a month or so away is scalding and needs immediate follow-up.

Quantity Question – Determining a prospect's potential volume of usage is often a key qualifier. UPS Brokerage, for instance, will determine the volume of packages being sent or received across the border to determine if it is worth the time and effort to follow-up.

Authority Questions – This is a good question to ask in some circumstances. Authority questions refer to who makes the decision, who is in charge, who are the key players, and to whom you should speak. This can save significant time and energy.

Budgetary Questions – Some companies will qualify on the basis of budget availability. If there is not budget money currently available, they might disqualify the client. Some firms swear by this question. They maintain that even if they have the right person and there is a definite need, if there is no budget, then there is no point. (Personally, I don't fully agree with this approach.)

Clincher Questions –This question won't apply to everyone, but it works well in the insurance industry. It looks something like this:

> **"Mr. Ebata, if we can provide you with a better premium and/or better coverage, is there any reason why you would not consider our insurance coverage."**

I like this question because it works very, very well. It boldly determines whether or not to pursue the lead further. The fact of the matter is that some clients will give you positive indications to your qualifying questions, but have absolutely no intention of considering your product or service offering. This phrase is a great disqualifier. See if you can use it.

TIP: How To Get the Right Questions

The best way to determine the right questions is to have a "Qualifying Question Workshop".

This was done at Cybermation Inc., the high-tech software company that I mentioned before. Cybermation has inside teams that take calls from, and make calls to clients and prospects. This team works with field reps spread across North America.

Bob Charendoff, the marketing manager, had the field sales team come together with the inside team to develop a series of qualifying questions that would suit the needs of the field rep. The workshop was interesting. The reps were asked to individually create a list of qualifying questions that they would ask a prospect. They were asked to be brutal in determining the questions, yet, when they came together as a group, there were over 20 different questions that were placed on the board! 20!

After some discussion, they reduced the questions to 15. Still too much, particularly for an add-on situation. But, after much lively debate, the reps were able to boil down the qualifying questions to four. It was felt that if these four questions were answered, the field rep could legitimately call and pursue the lead further down the funnel. Would they have liked all the 15 or 20 questions asked? You bet. But it wasn't going to happen.

So here's what you need to do:

Assemble all those who will be affected by the lead generation program (inside sales, marketing, field sales, technical support...whomever). Do NOT exclude those who will be impacted by the leads

Break into separate groups and have each group come up with a basic list of qualifiers

List the questions on a board and then review each and every one of them. Ask yourself if this questions is "vital" or "good to have" or "nice to have". Use an "ABC" or a "1-2-3" system, but, whatever you do, rate them.

Get a consensus on the four or five questions you are going to ask.

Ask those who must follow-up on the leads this question: "If these questions are properly asked, will you pursue the leads to the fullest?"

If you do this simple workshop, your lead generation program will have a much greater chance of success. Trust me. Painful experience has revealed this to me and many others over the years.

The Four-Step Process

I'll bet you thought I had forgotten the Four-Step process!
No way. The same rules apply.

Step 1: Take the Initial Request

I bet this one didn't surprise you.

Again, we are looking at the lead qualification process as
an add-on application to an existing call or visit, not as a
separate and distinct venture. Handle the inquiry, or take
the order, or manage the complaint, or whatever first.
Make certain that you have taken care of the customer/
prospect's immediate needs before you qualify.

AND REMEMBER: Focus only on the lead generation and
qualification application. Don't pile on.

Step 2: Bridge to Your Offer (Request)

If you have read the previous chapters, then you will know
the importance of the bridge as a signal that a transition
is occurring in the call. It is not a bad idea to pad this
bridge a little. For instance,

> **"Mr. Davison, while I have you, I'm not quite
> sure if this applies to you, but there a chance
> that we might (...list benefit... e.g. save you
> money, increase productivity, reduce the
> hassle of...)."**

> **"Aimee, before we conclude, depending on
> your current situation, there is a strong pos-
> sibility that we might be able to (list bene-
> fit)."**

> **"Ms. Mowery, before we finish up, I was ana-
> lyzing your purchase history with us over**

**the last several months, and I have an idea
that might (list benefit...).''**

The ABC's Of a Qualifying Bridge

When I said "pad" the bridge, you can see that the pad-
ding consists of a benefit statement. For those of you who
are familiar with outbound prospecting, you'll recognize
that this transition phrase is very similar to a cold-call
opening statement. This was no coincidence. At this point
in time, you need to intrigue your clients. You need to
catch their attention and get them to listen. So let's review the "ABCs" of a lead qualification bridge for a moment:

> *A. Use the Name.* You might be tired of hearing
> This, but use the client's name. Apart from building
> and maintaining rapport, it gets them to listen
> carefully to the next couple of lines. This is a small
> but oh-so-significant tip.

> *B. Transition.* Use phrases like "before we finish
> up," "while I have you," "one more thing...," etc.
> Like using the client's name, these phrases further
> catch the attention of the listeners by alerting
> them that there is one additional point. In effect,
> they are poised for your last comment.

> *C. Benefit.* Here's where you need to spend some
> time and craft the benefit statement. Of course,
> your benefit statement will relate to the product/
> service for which you intend to qualify. Hey, by
> now you must know that people buy benefits.
> Tossing out the benefits of saving time and money,
> or reducing hassle, or increasing productivity, or
> improving delivery, or whatever gives the client a
> definitive reason to listen further and to ultimately
> answer your questions.

Step 3: Present Your Offer

There are two components to the offer. The first component is to explain what it is you wish to do. In this particular case, your "offer" is the request to ask some questions. The implication is that if you ask some questions and there is a fit, then the client derives the benefit. After you have stated your bridge, here's how you do it.

> **"What I would like to do is ask you three or four questions to determine if there is a possible fit. How does that sound?"**

I won't belabor the point. The offer is simple and easy to understand. The client knows precisely what you want to do and why.

I have added a confirmation question**: "How does that sound?"** Some trainers, sales reps and managers might argue that you should not ask this question because it sets you up for a "no". Indeed, at times, this will happen but by my books, the "no" becomes a qualifier (or disqualifier). It suggests that you might have crossed the tolerance line. If the client doesn't grant you the time, so be it.

However, you might wish to try the assumptive approach and simply launch into your questions. After all, the rapport has been established ,and assuming you have effectively handled the initial request, there is a good chance that the client is positively inclined. You choose.

The second component of the offer is the questions themselves. Once permission is received either audibly or implied, move quickly to the questions. In fact, don't hesitate. Don't clutter the moment. Some reps feel a bizarre, almost compelling need to further explain their intention, sputtering this and that. Resist it.

Step 4: Close or Advance

I don't like the word "close" in this context. It implies the selling of a product or service, when, in fact, you should be moving the client to the next step in the selling cycle. For that reason, I like the word "advance". Advance suggests forward movement.

The Two Results

Based on your qualifying questions, one of two things will become immediately apparent: the client is not qualified or the client is qualified and should be moved to the next stage.

Not Qualified

If the client does not qualify (and chances are a greater percentage won't be), here's all you have to say:

> **"Aimee, based on what you have told me, it looks as though there is not a fit for our productivity software at this time, but thank you for giving me the time."**

That's it. Short and sweet.

Qualified

If the client does qualify here's what you say:

> **"Aimee, based on what you have told me, our work scheduling software might have a significant impact on managing your job tasks more effectively. I believe it is something worth examining further."**

> **"What I would like to recommend is ... present your advance: literature sent, a meeting**

with a sales rep, a further phone call to discuss, etc. How does that sound?"

I love scripted "transition" phases. It makes sales dialogues much easier. In this case, I use two. The first is *" based on what you have told me..."* This summary phrase not only gets their attention, it "announces" your conclusion or analysis of the situation. Note also, there is a benefit contained in the summary. Notice, it does not attempt to further explain or describe the software. This is not the time nor the place for long explanations. Remember, we are at the end of the call and the tolerance factor plays a significant role.

The second little transition phrase is *"What I would like to recommend ."* Customers and prospects love recommendations. The word is consultative in nature and you should use it often. A recommendation is non-threatening, not pushy and clients become exceedingly receptive to your suggestion.

The recommendation is your advance. You must know precisely where you wish to move the client. Do you want to send more information? Do you want a sales rep to call? Do you wish to set up a telephone appointment to do a further needs analysis? All these options must be determined ahead of time.

The advance is concluded with a closing phrase: "How does that sound?" or something similar.   You need to get a "yes" or a "no".

Putting it Together

Here's a good example. Maria is a UPS representative who handles customs brokerage for cross border packaging. Several times a day packages will arrive that need clearing at customs but there is no broker indicated. Maria will call the recipient and explain that a parcel has arrived and ask if they have a broker who can do the paperwork. If there is no broker, UPS will handle it.

This is where the opportunity for a lead is created. Once the paperwork is out of the way, the conversation looks something like this.

> **"I'll have that shipped to you today, Mr. Worman. While I have you, I wonder if I could ask you a few questions that might help expedite any parcels you receive in the future. How does that sound?"**

If the customer says yes (and they all do), here is what Maria asks to qualify the lead.

> **"Mr. Worman, how many international packages do you typically receive on a monthly basis? Do you send packages internationally? How many? Do you see these numbers increasing at all?"**

Depending on the answers to the questions, Maria can determine if there is a possibility for opening account. Assuming there is, here's what happens.

> **"Based on what you have told me, it looks like there is a good chance that we can set up an account for you, which will take the time and hassle out of calling us every time you send or receive a package."**

> **"What I would like to do is fax you an application form and then, within the next 48 hours, one of our reps will call you and review your situation further. What is your fax number?"**

Easy as pie!

Objections Handling
The client might object at this point. If they have questions about your product or service, be prepared to handle them or defer them to someone who can help them. You might not be the resident expert on scheduling software. If that's the case, advise the client and explain that someone else can handle that.

But, sometimes, even if the client qualifies by *your* standards, they may not qualify by *their* standards. In other words, they may not wish to see your fancy brochure, meet with your rep, or take a follow-up call. They might quietly say "I am not interested" or "no thank you".

What should you do?

Modern sales wisdom suggests that these are "knee jerk" objections. These are objections that customers and prospects toss out in an effort to protect themselves from being "sold". If this were a regular prospecting call, a savvy rep would not crumble and fall, but would attempt to engage the client further to determine why there is the initial resistance.

In an add-on situation like this, I would recommend that you DO NOT use this tactic.

This little gem of a recommendation might cause terror in the hearts of most sales trainers. Whatever. Never, ever forget that your qualification of a lead comes at the end of a call or contact. This was an add-on. It was not the primary reason for the contact. By now, you are well aware of the tolerance factor and the role it plays. Don't test it.

You must look at the big picture. If you continue to lengthen the call and pursue the lead, most clients grow tired and annoyed. This could have an impact on future calls to your company. If every call for an order or an inquiry is followed by a lengthy discourse, you run the risk of losing the client. That's a fact.

It is perceived as "harassment".

Don't do it.

Trouble Shooting
A generated lead does not necessarily turn into a sale .

Inevitably, I hear this phrase uttered from time to time: "We have tried to implement an add-on lead generation program and it doesn't work." Here is a list of things that typically impact the success or failure of the program.

Make Sure You Have the Right Question
Meet with the entire team as mentioned before. Review your questions. Are they getting the right type of information? Revamp and revise the wording if necessary. Test and learn.

Ensure Immediate Fulfillment
One thing that definitely plagues the lead generation/ qualification process is slow fulfillment. If literature is requested, fax, e-mail or mail it IMMEDIATELY. Strike while the prospect is hot. All too often, the material arrives weeks later and the prospect has forgotten. UPS faxes the form within 24 hours.

Ensure Immediate Follow-up
If the lead goes to a field sales rep, a follow-up contact MUST be made within 48 hours. Study after study reveals that sales closing rates increase proportionately the sooner the contact is made. The longer you take in following up, the less chance of closing…Gee, go figure that one.

I use the 48-hour policy. It says that whoever is making the follow-up call, whether an inside rep or a field rep, must do so within 2 working days of the initial contact with the client. I am saying there must be a visit or a

Dialogue, but rather some sort of immediate contact such as a voice mail, a message, or an e-mail.

Why 48 hours? Well, I tried four days and it inevitably lengthened itself to six or seven. I went to three and the follow-up took five. I went to two and the follow-up is usually done within 72 hours. You learn a thing or two with experience.

Customer Service "Contact"

Now, if you really want to ensure that the lead gets followed up on time, have an inside person call the customer within 72 hours of the initial contact. The call is positioned as a "customer service" follow-up call. It goes something like this:

> **"Oh yes, Mr. Worman, it's Greg Lopez at UPS Customer Service. The reason for my call today was to get some feedback on your experience at UPS brokerage and to see if you had an opportunity to speak with our accounts rep."**

Fields sales reps often get enraged when this program is implemented. I would hear cries like "You're checking up on us." For a while, a couple of years actually, I denied this, and explained the customer service benefits of the approach.

I don't bother with that excuse anymore.

I simply say "Yep!"

Many a field rep detested me and the control I placed on them, and guess what? Every single time the program was implemented and the reps were "made" to follow-up, closure rates were typically 30% higher than normal. Many of the reps still complain... and they still detest me all the way to the bank.

You don't have to do this. But I highly recommend it.

Feedback Loop
You must have a feedback loop to the reps who are generating the leads. If the leads are not effective, have a meeting. Review the questions. Revamp and revise as necessary.

Check individual results and compare. Sometimes one lead generator is more effective then another. Determine why. Sometimes some field reps will close at twice the rate of others. Determine why.

Summary
If you haven't considered an add-on lead generation/lead qualification program, now is the time to do it. Think it out. Plan it out. And do it.

Chapter 13

Selling On the Collection Call

How to Get Your Money,
Keep the Customer Happy and Still Sell More

Not every sales reps or customer service rep is responsible for collecting overdue accounts. Be glad for that. Collections for most people are not fun. But, if you do collect either in an official or unofficial capacity and you're looking to add some variety in your calls, then this chapter is for you. It's about doing more than simply getting the check.

You would think that just collecting the money was enough. You would think that there isn't really an opportunity to add-on sell.

Think again.

There are some circumstances in collections where you can add-on sell. This chapter focuses on how to "sell" more from those who owe you money. As you will see in two or three examples, there are a few companies and individuals who take a more entrepreneurial approach to collections. They have come   to learn that some collection calls are a great of opportunity to sell solutions or to sell more product. This not only makes the job more interesting and less frustrating for the collector, it also creates a stronger tie with the customer. In short, they can have their cake…and eat it too!

Last introductory point: this is not a chapter on "how to collect". There's books, tapes and seminars on that technique. This chapter has a much narrower focus. It is targeted to those customers who can and will pay. Once they are identified, add-on selling becomes easier and fun.

Three Types of Overdue Accounts

Let's check the collections playing field. There are really only three types of overdue accounts.

1. Those Who Can't Pay

For whatever reason, these are people or companies who simply don't have the financial resources to pay what is owed. In many cases, they want to pay but can't. Let's not worry about them because there is virtually no opportunity for an add-on sell.

2. Those Who Won't Pay

Again, for whatever reason, these customers refuse to pay. There could be bad blood, a major problem, revenge, an unethical mindset ...whatever. Here too, it is hard to apply the add-on sell. (I guess that's pretty obvious.)

3. Those Who Can Pay But Haven't

Here's the golden nugget. These are people or companies who have the money and who are willing to pay, but for some reason or another, they haven't. Here are some typical reasons why they have not paid.

- They forget

- They are disorganized

- Things got lost, misplaced etc.

- There is a problem/complaint they want resolved.

When you discover this third category of client, you have a darn good chance of applying an add-on selling application.

The Three-Step Process:
How to Sell On the Collection Call

You get a break on this technique because there are really only three steps instead of four. What a deal!

First, I am focusing on the third category of overdue accounts, those who can pay but haven't. I will not go into the process of how you do that other than to say that through questioning, experience, and gut feeling, you'll pretty much know which category you have. Ask any collector. They're savvy. If you're not experienced, don't fret. By the sound of the client's voice and by the words they use, you'll eventually be able to spot those who are legitimate and those who are not.

Anyway, let's start with the premise that you have someone who can pay and is willing to pay.

Step 1: Analyze The Cause

Let's start with an example that clearly illustrates the first step. BizGuard, Inc., is an alarm monitoring company that specializes in installing and monitoring alarm systems for the small businesses market. Maria LaForet is customer service rep, not a collector, whose job it is to contact those accounts that are overdue. Maria explains,

> *"Most of the small business accounts I deal with*
> *simply forget to send in the checks on a quarterly*
> *basis. We send out notices, of course, but they often*
> *get lost or misplaced or forgotten. I simply ask a*
> *few questions and I have learned that most of the*
> *time, the small businessman is doing ten things at*
> *once. The problem is time."*

Maria has learned that the customer has a problem: time.
Problems invite solutions.

Step 2: Present Your Offer and Benefit and Close

Here we are back to our old formula. You simply present
your solution and the benefit. This is typically what Maria
says:

> **"I understand your situation completely, Mr.**
> **Daley. I hear that from lots of small busi-**
> **nesses. Here's an idea for you to help you**
> **save time and hassle and to ensure that your**
> **alarm service is not interrupted...and you**
> **won't have to take any more calls from me.**
> **Why not send three postdated checks for**
> **$82.50 each, date them April 1, July 1, and**
> **October? Lots of our clients do just that.**
> **How does this sound?"**

Take a look at the offer. Maria has identified the problem
and presented a solution. The solution is to send three
post-dated checks. The benefit to the customer is a reduc-
tion in hassle, as well as the peace of mind knowing that
the alarm system will not be interrupted. While this is
presented as a collections call, it is really a sales call.

By the way, you would think that this simple solution
would be obvious for most businesses and you would
think that they would simply write postdated checks at
the beginning of the year and be done with it. It's not and

they don't. BizGuard has learned that small business firms don't usually run this way. This simple solution is often seen as a thunderbolt revelation from the sky…a way to free up time and reduce the hassle. Most of Maria's clients jump on board. (And those who don't typically are in a tight cash flow situation and this gives her a warning that the client might move from "can pay" to "can't pay".)

Step 3: Advance

The last step is somewhat different from our other applications. I call it the "Advance". An advance has three elements to it, and they are particularly critical in the collections game.

- The first element is that a *specific action* must be taken by the client.

- The second element is that there must be a *specific time frame* in which the action will take place.

- And third, the client must *agree* to the previous, to the action, and to the timeframe.

Using the example above, assuming Daley agrees with Maria's offer, the BizGuard advance looks like this.

> **"That's great Mr. Daley. So, you'll be writing a check for the current amount due which is $82.50 and that covers January, February and March. You'll also enclose three more checks for the same amount for April 1st, July1st and October 1st. If you write those checks today and get them in the mail, I should have them by Thursday. Will you do that?"**

The advance is critical. Don't skip it. Use it every time. Maria reviewed everything again so there was absolutely no confusion. She also "closed" the "sale" further by getting the client to agree to do it today.

NEAT TIP: Maria adds one more thing before closing. She says:

"Thank you Mr. Daley. I'll make a note in the file and mark Thursday in my calendar."

The remark is delivered casually, nicely and professionally. But it is also a subtle reminder that the commitment won't be forgotten or overlooked.

At this point, you might be thinking, "Hey, Jimbo, wait a minute: Is this REALLY a sale?"

Good question. Some will argue that this application isn't really a sale. The sale had been made.

Bull.

From where I sit, a sale isn't made until the money comes in. If you are on commission, you'll know what I mean. In BizGuard's case, the "sale" is getting the money that is owed and all future sums that come due. To BizGuard, this ensures cash flow, reduces the cost of reminder notices, and reduces the time and cost of collections. This means there is more time to track down those who really require a shove or two. Or, it frees up time to do other things: like sell. This means better profitability.

You bet it is a sale.

Up-Selling On the Collection Call

All right, you want an add-on selling situation in collections with a little more meat? How about up-selling on the collections call?

Compore.net is an Internet provider in Ottawa, Canada. Like many Internet providers, their service is based on the number of hours purchased: bronze, silver, gold and platinum. The bronze is the lowest number of hours and of course, the lowest price. At the opposite end of the spectrum lies platinum.

Melinda is a customer service rep who also collects past due accounts and can add-on sell like there's no tomorrow. I know. I'm her customer and I got a collections call. Quite honestly, I had no idea I was behind in my payment. (Honest!) What happened was that I did not see or I forgot to renew my yearly "gold" membership. It was due in November and along comes January. Not only was I behind in payment, but I was 126 hours over (Hey, cut me some slack, my 11-year old has discovered chat lines with a chat partner named Robin).

Melinda used the three-step process with me. Not only did she collect the overdue amount, she up-sold me to the platinum account. Here's what it looked like.

Step 1: Analyze

Melinda called and quickly explained that my account was overdue. I questioned and explained that I honestly did not know the account was late. I explained that the business was using the Internet far more now, that I had a web site and a weekly newsletter, (and a chatty son who logs on…often).

Bottom line for Melinda? My circumstances had changed. I required a different grade of service.

Step 2: Present Offer and Benefit
Recognizing that need, Melinda simply said,

> **"Mr. Domanski, I am not sure if you are aware of this, but we do have a Platinum membership. It gives you 3000 hours for $350.00/year. That should cover your needs and your son's too! We can apply the 126 hours against that."**

Heck, I didn't even know that there was a multi-level plan. And therein lies one of the key reasons why you can up-sell ... like I have said all along. The fact of the matter is that most customers don't know what you have to offer. Virtually any dialogue situation gives you the chance to educate, the chance to add-on sell.

Step 3: Advance
The good collector/customer service rep/sales rep Melinda advanced the sale with a simple line:

> **"We take Visa or Mastercard. Which would be better for you?"**

Gee, the oldest close in the book. And it is the oldest because it works.

Summary
For those customers who can pay and will pay, the opportunity to add-on sell exists to the same degree as those customers who place an order. You simply have to recognize the opportunity.

Chapter 14

Add-On Selling On The Service/Help Desk Call

People tend to trust service people and help desk providers. They are not seen as "sales people" so their recommendations are seen more as "value added consulting" and less as "pitching" a product. Because of this, people listen and respond favorably. If you are not using your service department or help desk to sell more products or services, then you are missing huge revenue opportunities.

In this chapter, we'll look at how you can leverage the calls to your help desk and service departments. We'll look at how the Four-Step Process can be quickly and easily applied to the benefit of the customer and the service/help desk rep. We'll also look at why help desk and service people resist the notion of "selling" and how to manage it.

It's fun, it's easy and it's profitable!

The Service and Help Desk Opportunity
A call made to a service department or help desk is similar to a complaint call, but without the complaining tone. To put it plainly, a service/help desk call is a first cousin to the complaint call and shares most the same characteristics.

The concept of selling on a service/help desk call is really quite simple. It boils down to this: The customer has a problem with their product or service. They call to have it fixed. They are looking for a solution. If they get it, they're satisfied. And when they are satisfied, they tend to be VERY open to the add-on sell.

There are three reasons for this and it is important that you understand them. If you truly understand the reasons why the add-on works, it helps make the process of adapting a selling concept easier.

1. Trust

People (customers) tend to trust service reps and help desk employees. Why? Because they are not seen as sales people. I can't explain it more simply than that. And as much as the facts might hurt, let them: generally speaking, customers tend to be leery about most sales reps. There is an innate fear of "being sold". As a sales-person, I don't like the implications of that message, but I accept it as human nature and do the best I can to make the selling experience a positive event.

That being said, many customers and prospects have a natural resistance to anyone in a selling situation. But that is rarely the case with service /help desk reps. There is a greater degree of trust because these reps are not seen as have a "hidden agenda". Customers see service and help desk representatives as helpers and problem solvers. Typically, they see any solution provided by the rep as a means of rectifying a situation. That's a positive. Leverage that trust. Provided your offer makes sense, provided it is value-added, and provided it ultimately benefits the customer, use the moment to provide an add-on sell.

2. Receptive

Because customers see service reps and help desk employees as trustworthy, they are more receptive to any recommendation that is made. Herein lies the opportunity: customers do not intuitively resist the suggestions provided by the reps. They are open to having the problem solved. They listen! They are, in effect, fertile ground for an add-on selling opportunity.

3. Value Added

Lastly, any recommendation made by a help desk or service rep is generally seen as value-added. Any proposal made is regarded as an insider's tip that is designed to help the user get the very best out of their product or service. Customers like it. They like getting advice from experts who apparently have nothing to gain from it.

Resistance: The Five Bulls and One Truth

Okay, if there are three good reasons why customers positively respond to an add-on sell by service or help desk reps, then why don't we see the application more often? The primary reason is that service and help desk reps tend to resist the application. Before we can look at *how* to implement the add-on, it is vital to understand why reps are reluctant to apply it.

Reason 1: "I Am Not a Sales Person."
BULL.

The first reason why add-on selling is not seen more frequently is that the average service rep and help desk employee does not see himself or herself as a sales person. The fact if the matter is, ***everyone*** who interfaces with a customer or a prospect is, in effect, selling. They sell the company, they sell the image, they sell themselves and above all, they sell their solutions or advice. It is absolutely vital that a service person or help desk rep understand that every call they take or make is a selling situation.

Customers sit back and watch. They observe behavior. They listen closely. Every word, every nuance is carefully evaluated on a conscious or subconscious level. At stake is satisfaction. The rep is selling satisfaction. It might be an answer to a problem regarding a software glitch or it might be the repair of a toaster oven on Boxing Day (a Canadian holiday). If satisfaction is not obtained, a sale is lost. It might be a return of an item. It might be a loss of future sales. It might be bad word of mouth spread from one customer to another. So, make no mistake about it, these reps sell.

It is not a huge leap of faith to suggest that selling additional products is part of the job. If a customer needs a router for his computer network in order to share data from one computer to another, then it is the obligation of the service rep to recommend it. Label it in whatever manner you like, it is selling. Period.

What this really means is that, in the short run, you must educate your reps (or yourself) that any and every service or help desk rep is a sales person with a different title. In the long run, if you manage the department, you must begin to hire reps with the implicit understanding that selling is part of the job description.

Get over it.

You or your reps are sales people.

Reason 2: "I Don't Get Paid For It."
BULL.

You DO get paid for it.

If you are a service rep or help desk consultant, you are getting paid for assisting the customer. For solving problems. For fixing products. If solving a problem means making recommendations for additional products or services, so be it. You get paid for satisfaction. Satisfaction means solving problems and concerns by whatever means.

It also means recognizing that certain other products or services might enhance the value of the existing product or service. If you suggest this to the client, you are creating value. Value keeps customers coming back. It means more sales. It means referrals. You get paid for enhancing satisfaction.

Reason 3: "Customers Don't Like It."
BULL.

We looked at this earlier in the book. What customers dislike is shoddy and poorly delivered add-on recommendations. They dislike add-on suggestions that don't apply to their situation or their problem.

What they do like is anything that solves problems. What they like is anything that might make future problems less likely. What they like is peace of mind. What they like are tips, techniques and ideas that can make them more effective. What they like are options to consider.

While we're at it, let's get one thing straight so you don't think I am sugar-coating the application: Your solution or recommendation may not always please the customer. No one likes to fork out $500.00 for a repair. You know this and so do I. But if that's what is required, then it is the job of the service rep or help desk expert to deliver this message. Hiding this fact or avoiding it won't make the problem go away.

Once the painful news has been digested, the customer then wants to have some reassurance that it won't happen again. In some cases, it might be a warranty or a service agreement. Ask any furnace service person in northern Minnesota when he has to repair a unit when it is -40 degrees with wind chill. A customer will pay whatever it takes. They don't particularly like it, but they have little choice. If the serviceman can offer some sort of agreement that would remove this sting in the future, what is the worst the customer can say?

At this point, the customer has been educated. He or she has a choice to make. They can either say "yes" or "no". But, at least they know. That's value added. You can bet your bottom dollar that the customer will be a heck of a lot happier if the furnace fails again when it is -52 degrees and he has an agreement.

Reason 4: "It Doesn't Work."
BULL.

This myth has been created by those who don't particularly want to apply add-on selling.

I don't have statistics on how well the application works or doesn't work. I wish I did. But simple logic and personal experience suggest it can and does work. I have called help desks on my computer and service departments on furnaces, stoves and dishwashers. I have paid for repairs and have bought additional products that might help enhance a situation. I bet you listen to your service person. I bet you see the help desk person as a savior and a saint when he or she helps you recover your entire database.

But, here's what you need to understand:

> *For the amount of time and effort it takes to recommend an add-on sell, the return on investment is significant.*

175

Reason 5: "I Don't Have the Time."
BULL.

Let's put this little ditty to bed once and for all: It takes less than 30 seconds to make a recommendation or a suggestion.

You have the time.

Period.

End of discussion.

Reason 6: "I Don't Know How."
Ahhhhh...now *this* is a different story. No BULL here. Service and help desk reps are hired for their knowledge and expertise for analyzing, fixing, repairing and helping. Their training is usually focused on these areas. Very few have been taught how to sell...or should I say, how to *effectively* sell. All too often, an executive or manager gets a notion that the help and service people can sell and issues an edict that says, "Oh, by the way, make sure you tell them about the service agreement."

And that's the extent of the training.

I am certain that some reps actually give it a shot. They "tell" the customer about a service agreement with little or no explanation. The customer says no thanks to the offer. The reps are discouraged, maybe even embarrassed. They stop telling the customer. Few, if any, agreements are sold. The conclusion? Add-on selling doesn't work.

What is so often missing are the skills and techniques for delivering a meaningful add-on message. Thank goodness for the Four-Step Add-on Selling Process.

The Four-Step Add-On Selling Process for Service/Help Desk Reps

Selling doesn't have to be hard or painful. It can be quite rewarding for the rep, the customer and the company. Like most of the other applications in this book, selling on the service call or help desk is a matter of four simple steps.

Step 1: Handle the Initial Problem/Concern

The first, and most obvious step is to handle the customer's problem or concern. If someone calls your help desk to say that they cannot log into their cash register and there are sixty customers lining up, you need to get that problem fixed. Pronto. If you're a furnace repairperson in International Falls, Minnesota or Fort Frances, Ontario, and it's -41 degrees outside and your client's furnace is not working, fix it. Double pronto.

No one cares about your offer until his or her immediate needs are met. Enough said.

Step 2: Bridge to the Add-On

Understand one thing: You cannot bridge to an add-on sell until the customer is satisfied. In other words, if you have not fixed the cash register or the furnace DO NOT bother to mention the add-on offer...

...*unless* the solution to the problem lies in the offer. Most help desk and service people are familiar with this situation. Sometimes the only solution is to buy a part. I don't see that as an add-on sell. I see that as a necessity. The customer really has no choice, so it is not an add-on.

But, assuming that the customer's needs are satisfied, you have the opportunity to add-on sell. The bridge is a simple step that tells the customer you are moving to another area of discussion. In effect, it serves as a pre-text for the add-on. Here are some phrases you can use:

"Mrs. Ruelle, if you have a moment..."

"Mr. Bothwell, while I have you..."

"Trudi, I have an idea..."

"Steve, you might be interested in..."

"Sabrina, there is something you should consider..."

TIP

Use the Customer's Name

Notice how the bridge uses the customer's name.

Why?

Two reasons. First, it gets the attention of the customer. Studies show they tend to listen to the next 8-10 words very closely. Since the next step is to present the offer, you want your client to be focused on your add-on sell. The closer they listen, the easier it is.

The second reason is that using the name creates a small bond; a sense of relationship, however small. This is important. I have dealt with service repair people and help desk staff for years. It is a rare thing to hear them use my name in a conversation (unless you know them through multiple calls). There is a general reluctance to use names. This creates a bit of a barrier between individuals. Used sincerely and in context, a name helps warm up the relationship to the extent that the customer will focus a little more intently on your offer. Hey, it's small, but a lot of small things make a big thing...like a sale.

Step 3: Present Your Add-on And Benefit
Choose your add-on.

Is it a cross-sell of a product or service that will make the problem go away for good or ease the financial pain if it occurs again? Is the add-on a lead generation question sequence that might lead to a bigger sale. For instance, the customer needs an entire new computer system. Maybe a field or inside sales rep should be reviewing the customer's situation. Do you want to gather some market intelligence to enhance future products?

The trick is to be prepared ahead of time. If you're company has a special promotion on a product or service, make sure you a familiar with it. In any case, assuming you have an add-on offer, present it. Make it perfectly clear so there is not confusion.

> **"Mrs. Ruelle, if you have a moment, I have a suggestion that might take the sting out of the next service call. It is called our "No Hassle Service Agreement."**

> **"Mr. Bothwell, while I have you, you might want to consider upgrading your video card..."**

> **"Trudi, I have an idea that could reduce the problems you're having with transmitting documents..."**

Then, next step is to explain the offer and provide a benefit.

TIP

Use Simple Language

One of the secrets of selling on a service or help desk call is to use simple language when explaining your offer. The explanation tells the customer what the add-on offer will do for them; how it will solve a problem; how it will make them more effective; how life can be easier, faster, simpler...whatever.

The explanation of the offer is absolutely, positively vital and it is something with which many service reps and help desk reps sometimes have difficulty. Service and Help Desk reps lose many opportunities because their explanations or suggestions are cluttered with technical jargon. The average customer is bewildered and lost.

This is understandable, of course. Calls to help desks and service departments tend to be related to things technical. Something doesn't work. Most often, the solution is a technical in nature. The rep, being technically driven, gives technical answers that few people understand. This is why it is important to prepare ahead of time. Have a script that simplifies the offer.

To continue the examples above,

> **"Mrs. Ruelle, if you have a moment, I have a suggestion that might take the sting out of the next service call. It is called our "No Hassle Service Agreement". For less than $10.00 per month, all parts and labor are covered should your furnace break down. This means you don't pay a thing...ever."**

> **"Mr. Bothwell, while I have you, you might want to consider upgrading your video card. What this will do is allow you to play your "Star Trek: Dominion Wars" at higher skill levels without the freezes and crashes. It is only $126.00 plus shipping."**

"Trudi, I have an idea that could reduce the problems you're having with transmitting documents. If you were to install a ZIP drive, you could, in effect, make your documents smaller when send them across the Internet. Your investment in the drive is only $xx... and it will reduce the hassle and frustration that you are currently experiencing."

```
TIP

Make Sure You Add a Benefit
```

If you are not in sales, the term "benefit" may not be familiar to you. A benefit is what the customer ultimately derives from the purchase of a product or a service. A customer may be buying a ZIP drive which is inserted into a computer, but the real benefit they are buying is the freedom from hassle. Mrs. Ruelle may get a piece of paper for her No Hassle Service Agreement, but the real benefit she derives is not paper and words, but rather peace of mind. Mike Bothwell benefits by having the sheer joy of defeating the Dominion rather than the shear frustration of not being able to save the Alpha Quadrant.

So, the point here is, you must explain what the offer does and how it will benefit the customer because you must assume the customer does not know what you know. Look at how empty these phrases are without an explanation.

"Mrs. Ruelle, if you have a moment I would like to recommend our "No Hassle Service Agreement". Do you want it?"

**"Mr. Bothwell, while I have you, you might
want to consider upgrading your video
card. Shall I do that?"**

**"Trudi, I'd like to suggest you install a ZIP
drive. What do you think?"**

These offers are groovy and smashing **if** the customer
knows what the Agreement, video card and ZIP drive are
all about. But I'll bet most people don't. I don't. Look at
those offers carefully. Would you take the rep up on the
offer? No. I didn't think so.

Customers are starved for information. Good information.
They want to be educated. They want a consultant. Be
one.

Step 4: Close

The final step is very important and is so often ignored.
It is called the "close". Translated, the close is a question
that gets the customer to take some sort of action to buy
or not to buy.

Why should you close?

Because, most customers won't close themselves. They
need a little help; a gentle push. You should also close because it saves time. A direct question will either yield a
"yes", a "no" or an objection. If it is "yes", well, you've got
a sale. If it is "no", you move on. No sweat. If there is an
objection (question) answer it. It helps the customer make
a decision one way or the other.

So, ask things like:

"Would you like to proceed?"

"What do you think?"

"How does that sound to you?"

"Shall we proceed?"

"Would you like me to add that to the invoice?"

"What would you like to do?"

"We take Visa or MasterCard?"

"Would you like us to bill you?"

You get the picture

FINAL TIP: Practice.

If you are in service or if you work on a help desk, chances Are, you have not had much experience in selling. When you read the four steps and look at the examples, chances are, they make you a tad bit uncomfortable. That's okay. They are new to you. New things make most of us feel uncomfortable. But they do work and they work well.

What you need to do to get over the awkwardness of the approach is to practice. Practice it on your spouse, your kids, co-workers, your boss, or strangers. (Just kidding about the strangers.)

FINAL, FINAL TIP for Managers and Executives:
Compensate.

If you are an executive or manager of a help desk or a service department, you might want to consider compensating your reps for each sale the make. It doesn't have to be much, but it should recognize their effort. Selling takes some time and effort. There is a risk of rejection at some level. So, it is important that the effort is rewarded in some manner.

Summary
Perhaps the biggest selling opportunity for non-sales people lies in the area of service and help desks. With a little thought and exploration, you have a tremendous opportunity to add-on sell to the benefit of your customer, your company and you.

Chapter 15

Add-On Selling
On the Internet

This will be a short chapter, but it is vitally important. It will be short simply because I am not an expert on the Internet. It is still an emerging industry and besides, there are experts who are far more knowledgeable than me on this topic. But, in the same breath, it does not take a whack with a huge stick to realize that the Internet is growing and will have a profound impact on marketing and sales (even if the whole dot com boom had kind of dwindled on the vine).

The Internet Importance in Add-On Selling
The Internet is important for the following reasons.

- The Internet is becoming a predominant force in communication. Certainly, e-mails have impacted the way we communicate around the world from businesses to consumers. You can't ignore the medium if only because of its sheer size and scope. You can't ignore it because purchasers, key decision makers, executives...heck, everyone is using it.

- The Internet is supplementing how we market and sell are products. The e-commerce craze did not really blossom like many thought it would, but as a sales support tool and even as a direct selling medium for many businesses, it is now a vital element in the sale and marketing process.

- The Internet attracts a different prospect and customer. This IS important. Studies in various markets and various industries reveal that those who surf, shop and communicate via the Internet are a different breed of cat than would typically call an 800 line or visit a retail shop or business. More educated? More curious? More passive, yet more informed, this is a whole new market niche for many industries. You can't ignore them…nor can you ignore their potential.

- Because of software and other Internet technology, a business or sales rep can add all sorts of attachments to their correspondence and communication with clients. PowerPoint presentations, audio clips, video images and Flash demos are just a few of the things that can add a whole new dimension to your selling activities.

- The Internet is important because telephone technology has made sales a more arduous process. I am talking about voice mail. If you're a field or inside sales rep making calls to your clients and prospects, you will know that about 60%-70% of the time, your calls will encounter voice mail. A 30%-40% penetration level is not the best of statistics. E-mail offers a way to supplement your selling activities.

So, that's Domanski's look at the Internet world. I am sure there are a dozen other perspectives. The point is, from an add-on selling perspective it might not be a bad idea to implement one or two strategies listed here and, at the same time, explore other opportunities.

The Add-On Opportunities
I'll make this real simple. There are two Internet opportunities: add-on selling through e-mail and add-on selling through web sites.

1. How to Add-On Sell with E-Mail

When you think about it, an e-mail is no different from a telephone conversation or a face-to-face conversation. For that matter, it is no different from direct mail. E-mail represents an opportunity to initiate and/or continue a dialogue with a client or prospect. So, that means we can apply the same principles of add-on selling.

❏ *Signature Files.* Here is an add-on technique that ANYONE can implement immediately. It's a great way to leverage your e-mail and do some add-on selling. It's called a signature file. A "sig file" is like an e-business card. It is something that can be added to the end of your e-mail not unlike a postscript. Because it comes at the end of your e-mail, it is perfectly positioned for an add-on sell.

Here's my sig file:

****

Jim Domanski
Teleconcepts Consulting
Tele-Sales Consulting, Training and Keynotes
1 888 353 0948
www.teleconceptsconsulting.com

To subscribe to the complimentary weekly Tele-sales Vitamins just reply to this message with "subscribe" in the subject line.

****

Do you remember the two reasons why people don't buy more? One reason is that they don't know you have the product/service for sale, and the other is that you don't tell them.

What this sig file does is tells readers of my e-mails that I do consulting, training and keynotes. I communicate what I do. I also link them to my web site so they can see more. And I have also added a "cross-sell" with reference to the Tele-Sales Vitamins weekly e-newsletter. While I do not derive a fee for the service, I still see this as a cross-sell because I have yet another medium to educate readers about my products and service.

The sig file is a simple, yet powerful method of implementing an add-on sell, but it seems to be ignored.

I proved this to myself about a half-an-hour or so ago. I scanned my inbox and reviewed eight e-mails from existing vendors who sell to my company. Not one, *not one* single e-mail had a signature file whatsoever.

The sig file is typically permanent. In other words, when the e-mail is sent, the sig file goes out automatically. You don't have to think about it, which is a good thing. But again, it is permanent which means that whatever add-on selling application you apply must be constant.

❏ *The Footer.* A Footer is not unlike a sig file in that it comes at "the foot" of an e-mail. An e-mail can have a series of footers divided by lines, which communicate a message or two.

Here's an example: Mark Sanford is a consultant who sent an e-newsletter called Coldcalling.com Newsletter. At the end of the article he has the following footers:

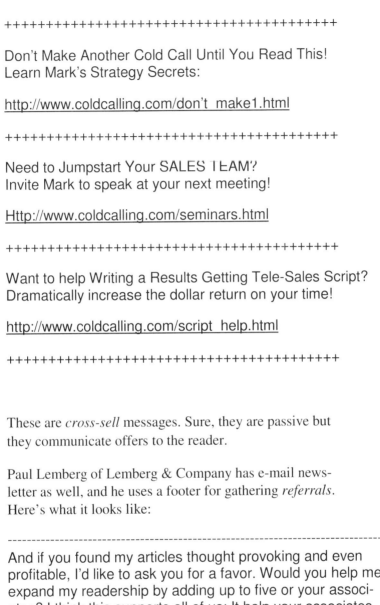

++

Don't Make Another Cold Call Until You Read This!
Learn Mark's Strategy Secrets:

http://www.coldcalling.com/don't_make1.html

++

Need to Jumpstart Your SALES TEAM?
Invite Mark to speak at your next meeting!

Http://www.coldcalling.com/seminars.html

++

Want to help Writing a Results Getting Tele-Sales Script?
Dramatically increase the dollar return on your time!

http://www.coldcalling.com/script_help.html

++

These are *cross-sell* messages. Sure, they are passive but they communicate offers to the reader.

Paul Lemberg of Lemberg & Company has e-mail news-letter as well, and he uses a footer for gathering *referrals*. Here's what it looks like:

And if you found my articles thought provoking and even profitable, I'd like to ask you for a favor. Would you help me expand my readership by adding up to five or your associ-ates? I think this supports all of us: It help your associates by making them aware of a source of new and useful ideas. It helps me, by expanding the list of people I reach with my writing. It helps you---well, you get to do someone a favor, and a valuable favor at that.

Lemberg's approach is effective for two notable reasons. First, he uses a chatty, almost colloquial method of communicating. You get the feel he is on the phone with you or sitting in front of you. This tends to make the add-on more natural. Second, Lemberg uses benefits to help sell the referral. He points out the win/win/win scenario that occurs with the referral, with the reader and with Lemberg himself.

So, when you analyze it, Lemberg is really using the Four-Step Approach to Add-On Selling: First, he provides the message (i.e., the content of the newsletter). He bridges to the referral with a neat little phrase: "And if you found my articles thought provoking..." It is not unlike saying "Mr. Needham, while I have you..." He then clearly states the add-on with the benefit. Good stuff!

❏ *The Header.* While the Add-On formula I present throughout the book places the add-on proposition at the END of a call, with an e-mail things can be a little different. You can place the add-on at the BEGINNING of a call. It's clever in a way. Think about it. You can't really get to the substance of an e-mail without first encountering the header. It's there in front of you.

Art Sobczak's T*elE-Sales Hot Tips of the Week* e-newsletter starts off like this:

```
================================
```
Please forward these Tips to a friend who could benefit from them, or have them send us a message with JOIN in the subject. Or, go to <http://www.businessbyphone.com/backissues.htm> to join online, where you can also see the recent Volume 4 back issues free. To leave this list, reply with REMOVE in subject line.
```
================================
```

This is an absolute classic cross-sell message on several levels. Note how he asks for referrals by asking the reader to forward the message on to a friend. Or, they could join by going to his back issues page, where he has the benefit, "Free". The cross-sell comes when people see the current back issues, they can also **buy** the other back issues. And Art tells me they do, in great numbers.

Other Header Applications

The easiest and perhaps most applicable add-on applications for e-mails (and particular, e-newsletters) is cross-selling. We've already seen Paul Lemberg (among others) use e-mail to gather referrals. But Lemberg is imaginative enough to use his header for a couple of other applications: market intelligence and lead generation.

A while ago, I received Paul's e-newsletter and the header invited the reader to complete a survey about strategic issues in management. The offer also explained that the results would be shared with those who participate. It sounded fair enough to me, so I participated. As I completed the survey, I recognized that while Lemberg gathered great data that could be used in his consulting practice, he was, at the same time, identifying leads for his services. Brilliant!!

❏ *Midders.* You've seen "Headers" and "Footers" now let's introduce "Midders." I don't know if the word "midder" exists. I doubt it because I just created it. Whatever the origin, I am using it to describe the use of a message (in this case, an add-on sell) "mid way" in the text.
I am seeing this crop up more and more. The reader is drawn into the text of the message and then somewhere sandwiched in the middle is an add-on sell. For instance, in my e-newsletter, Tele-Sales Vitamins, I might be writing an article on up- selling. I could be discussing the first two steps on the Four-Step Process when, suddenly, you see a quick message like this.

For More Information on up-selling and other revenue generating techniques, order "ADD-ON SELLING" by dialing 1-888-343-0948.

Then, the article would be completed with the final two steps.

This really a powerful way to get the message read. Footers and headers work well, but readers have a way of getting used to the technique and quickly dismissing the front and back ends of the e-mail. The midder is a little different. If the reader has been drawn into the text, it is difficult to ignore the midder.

❏ *The P.S.:* Okay, you don't do newsletters. You're "just" a sales rep or customer service rep. You simply send e-mails out in response to client or prospect requests. You may or may not add a sig file. You might be like me and you're useless at trying to create sig files or imbedding headers, footers and midders. (I get someone else to do that kind of stuff.) Is there anything else you can do to stimulate an add-on sell?

You bet.

What about a plain, old fashioned postscript? A good old "P.S." after you have typed in your name is STILL a powerful tool in the communication process. Ask any direct marketer. Anyone can do it...especially you. It is fast, easy and flexible AND uses the Four-Step Process.

The Four-Step Add-On Approach to E-mails
Step 1: Deal With the Customer Request
There could be any number of reasons why you would use
e-mails to contact your customers or prospects. Whatever
the reason, make sure you tackle the primary objective of
the e-mail first. The same reasons apply here as they do
in face-to-face or telephone situations.

Step 2: Bridge
What could be simpler? The bridge in this case is the P.S.
This comes at the very end of your message and after
your name. We consumers have been conditioned to the
P.S. for decades. It's a perfect bridge.

Step 3: Present Your Offer and Benefit
If you have an item on sale, describe it. If you have a sur-
vey you'd like them to complete, say so and explain why.
Hyerlink to a web site for completion. Toss in a benefit
for good measure. Lemberg is very effective in doing this.
Here are a few tips.

- Create your Offer and Benefit well ahead of time
  and use the "cut and paste" feature to apply it to
  your e-mails.

- Not all e-mails will lend themselves to a particular offer. Have multiple add-on offers if applicable.

- Use the person's name in the PS. For instance,

  *P.S. Mr. Edgerton, if you like our smoker-BBQ,
  you'll absolutely love our Smoker Accessory Pak.
  For just $19.95 you'll get a heapin' helpin' bottle of
  JIMBO Serious Steak Seasoning, a box of hickory
  chips, ARTERO's Secret BBQ Sauce, and Famous*
  Freddy's Old South Rib Rub. Time Limited: Visit

our web site _____ or call _____. Guaranteed to
make an everyday BBQ a sensation.

Step 4: The Close
Well, it's hard to close when an e-mail, by its nature, is a
monologue. However by urging the reader to take action
and by adding "Time Limited", a certain sense of urgency
is created.

Simple, but oh, so effective.

Two Web Sites and Add-On Selling
I am not going to spend too much time on add-on selling
other than to give a couple of simple examples. I am not a
web expert and besides, visiting a web site is not exactly a
one-to-one type of selling or customer service relationship, unlike e-mail. But, I wanted to address it only because the opportunity for an add-on sell exists and the potential is strong.

In surfing web sites, it is clear there are two approaches
to add-on selling. One approach is subdued. In other
words, the add-on sell is discrete. A good example is
Franklin Covey Canada. If you visit their web site,
www.franklincovey.ca, and begin to browse their products,
you'll discover a boxed text at the bottom of each description that looks like this:

> **Be sure to order a Storage Case for easy access to
> past and future planner pages.**

This text box is a permanent feature on the web page.
Nothing terribly fancy, but it fits with the positioning and

style of the company. It is a good cross-sell. It educates the visitor, it comes at the end of the product description, and there is an implied benefit ("easy access").

Paul Lemberg & Company, as we have seen, is a little more high tech. Recently, I signed up for an e-training course provided by Lemberg. After I completed the registration and payment form and hit "enter," a pop-up text box zipped out onto the screen. It featured a small blurb on one of his books. A hyperlink took you to a description of the book and, of course, it allowed you to add it to your shopping cart.

So, think about it for a moment. Lemberg has clearly and effectively mastered the concept of add-on selling in a more inactive way than most. As in a telephone call to an order desk, the initial sale is taken. That's step one in the Four-Step Process. The pop-up menu occurs immediately afterwards and, of course, serves as the "bridge". That's Step 2. The third step is the product description and benefits are clear and concise while the "close" comes with the words "add to the shopping cart". The customer cannot proceed without at least seeing the message. It's classic stuff and very good.

Ever been to Las Vegas and drove around? There are flashing lights, neon lights, billboards, big statues, noise blaring…you name it. All these devices are struggling to get through the clutter and get your attention. At first, you try to absorb it all, but it is impossible. In fact, it is down-right overwhelming and annoying. After a while, the garishness becomes a part of the scenery and ignored.

As a consumer and web surfer, that's how I see many web sites. Some web sites have a loud, add-on selling presence. At some point, I am sure you have come across a web site that has banners, flashing icons, racing arrows and every other gimmick under the sun. It becomes oppressive. You cannot keep up with the messages that are bombarding you. And in that context, the add-on selling is essentially lost.

Summary: Less is More
An obvious lesson: Less is more.

If you have a web site or you use e-mail, recognize that you have a powerful medium by which to add-on sell. By all means, leverage the medium. At the same time, recognize that the more you cram into the medium, the less it will be read. For instance, I receive several e-newsletters. Some have become so cluttered with headers, footers and midders that it is difficult to find the text. The text represents the reason for my being there. I think many authors have forgotten this. Consequently, I see the newsletter as nothing more than a classified ad section from a newspaper in electronic format. Bottom line? It doesn't get read. The text isn't read and certainly the add-on message are not read.

Use the add-on opportunity that the Internet provides wisely. One or two or three messages, placed strategically is far more effective than a dozen competing with one another. These messages will get read and will not interfere with the primary objective or your web site or e-mail.

Chapter 16

Down-Selling
(When Selling Less Is Selling More)

Just when you thought it was safe to apply add-on-selling and increase revenues ... along comes down-selling.

This short, but important chapter is about a technique or approach called down-selling. In a way, it is the opposite of add-on selling. This chapter examines down-selling in more detail and looks at the special circumstances where selling less is actually selling more. A down-sell is a way to save a customer. A down-sell is a way to create more sales in the future. A down-sell is a way to add-on sell.

Interested? Confused?

Well, read on and see what down-selling can do for you.

Down-selling Defined
What a better way to start than with a good clear definition:

> *Down-Selling is the process of offering an alternative product or offering a lower price in order to make a sale, save a sale or ensure future sales.*

You read that right. At a *lower* price than the customer might have anticipated. As mentioned, it would appear to be the opposite of everything this book purports to be. E-gads, you say? Has Jim gone off the deep end?

Not really.

In truth, down-selling is not so much a technique as it is common sense. In some cases, as you will see, the bottom line is that *something* is better than *nothing*.

When to Use Down-Selling

An important word here: It is vital to completely understand that down-selling comes at the END of the call. Like all the add-on applications listed in the book, it comes only after you have analyzed the situation. You don't set out to down-sell a customer or a prospect. It is NOT your primary objective.

The down-sell is a back-up strategy. Your fallback position. Something you hold in reserve. More on this in the section entitled "The Down-Sell Danger", but for now, just remember that you use the technique at the end of your call.

Three Ways to Use Down-Selling

1. To Make a Sale

The first down-sell application relates to making a sale. Sometimes people have their heart set on one item but they can't get it. Either it is too expensive or it is unavailable or whatever. But that doesn't mean there aren't alternatives that might suit the customer's needs. Remember, the customer has already made up his or her mind to buy. The tough part is over. The propensity to spend is at a maximum. You have a choice: you can let the customer walk or you can offer an alternative.

Here's a perfect example. Greg Colbert is a sales rep that works for Affymetrix, a biotechnology firm. Affymetrix fields numerous calls from the academic community regarding their innovative technologies. Most the technology is leading edge and carries with it a heavier price tag, particularly for budget-strapped institutions.

Greg will get calls from the academics wishing to purchase the technology, but who quickly become unsettled when the price is presented. Like many companies who sell to the academic community, the budget IS the budget. Finding additional sources of capital is difficult at the best of times.

But rather than let the prospect hang up, Greg takes the time to question the caller and determine the type of research being conducted. Often Affymetrix will have an older technology which will satisfy the caller's requirements. Greg presents the solution and often gets a sale, even though the price of the unit might be significantly less than the new technology.

Tips

- For the down-sell to work in your organization, you must be a product knowledge expert. You need to know your products inside and out and what differentiates each.

- You also need to be an expert at questioning to assess the client's needs.

- Job aids can help. Have a chart that shows the flow of top-of- the- line models right down to the bottom-of-the-line models. This is a handy, easy to use reference that allows you to quickly shift product gears.

2. Prevent a Cancellation
The second way to use down-selling is with an existing client who wants to cancel an order or a subscription. There are three of angles here:

The Lower Price Down-Sell. Clement Communications sells posters and other communications programs that focus on safety, security, quality control, team spirit and a host of other applications. The company has been around since the 1920's and makes a superb product that is designed to create awareness through visual communications. (If you have ever seen the "Herman" Safety Posters, you have seen Clement.)

The programs are on a subscription basis and as with any Subscriptions, cancellations occur from time to time. But Clement has learned that some of the programs can be salvaged. Here's what they do.

A rep will call the cancelled subscriber and ask why the program was cancelled. Most clients are quite straightforward. Sometimes, the newsletter or poster doesn't apply anymore. We saw that in the "Cancellations" chapter. Sometimes, the issue is price. As I write this, there is an economic turndown. Businesses slash as many expenses as they can. Knowing this, but also knowing the value of the program to most organizations, the Clement rep will sometimes offer a discount. For instance,

> **"Mr. Potter, if we could reduce the subscription price by, say 10%, could you maintain the subscription?"**

Remarkably, a percentage of subscribers can justify the investment by having a little nudged off. For Clement, it means a smaller margin, but compared to the cost of acquiring a new customer, the amount is insignificant.

The Value-Added Down-Sell. Continuing with Clement as an example, the rep has an alternative to reduce the price of the subscription. The strategy is to increase the value of the product for the price that is paid. So, on some occasions, the down-sell offer might look like this:

> **"Mr. Dumbledore, if we could add an additional poster on either quality or teamwork to help supplement the safety posters, could you maintain the subscription?"**

This is another superb way of keeping the client rather than losing the client. Clement gives a little by creating more value to justify the price. This is something that most clients can sink their teeth into.

Other companies will offer a "free" special report or a book or any number of items as an enticement for the client to remain. Somewhere down the line, it costs the company something and that's why it is a down-sell. But, as mentioned, the benefits are greater than losing the client completely.

The Alternative Product Down-Sell. The third angle to the down-sell is the alternative product. This is not unlike the applications of saving a sale through a down-sell except that you have an existing client.

The best example of this was demonstrated in the "Can-Collations" chapter where sales rep Patrick Hennessy of Australia offers an alternative product for their book summaries.

Similar to Greg Colbert at Affymetrix, Patrick analyzes the customer's needs to determine why the product was being cancelled. He discovers, for instance, that many of the subscribers want a more focused book summary. Instead of getting book summaries on leadership plus sales and marketing, some executives want just leadership summaries. The sales and marketing are of no value. Patrick's approach is to offer summaries of leadership only. In specific cases like these, Hennessy down-sells and saves as many as 50% of those who call to cancel. Not bad!

3. You Down-Sell When it Buys
You Sell More in the Long Run
The final application of a down-sell scenario is a little bit more strategic in nature. You down-sell when you know that future sales are likely on the line. This is a real judgment call and a leap of faith because it implies you

can make a big sale now and be happy, but you can lose future sales.

Let's go to Oak Bay Marina, the British Columbia vacation company that sells top-of-the-line sport fishing packages to the discerning fisherman...and his family. Oak Bay has a long-term view of its clients. It sees them as repeat customers and sources of referrals and good will ("walking, talking advocates"of their resorts). They know that by not making as much on one particular sale, could very likely mean making *more* on future sales.

There three reasons or benefits as to why Oak Bay will down-sell:

First, when Oak Bay Marina telesales reps like Jason Guille take calls from fishermen from around the world, they know right off the bat that if the experience for the fishermen is powerful, they'll be back. In fact, over 50% of the time, the visitors to Oak Bay Marina will come back. They've learned this over time. They've learned that by selling the right package at the right time means a repeat customer.

The second reason for the down-sell is that Oak Bay has learned that when repeat visitors do come back, they tend to want to try more or experience more. They are extremely receptive to up-sell and cross-selling because the trust has been established. In other words, the customers buy more the second time around. That's when add-on selling really kicks in.

The third reason is that these customers tend to give referrals and leads. And why wouldn't they? The experience was so positive from stem to stern that a name or two is not unusual. This means more sales down the line.

The Down-Sell Danger–The Under-Sell

Be careful! You must use the down-sell wisely. Confusion sometimes arises when down-selling. The down-sell sometimes gets muddled with the "under-sell."

Let me explain. For some reps, there is a strong temptation to under sell, which is a whole lot different from a down-sell. An under-sell is simply a cheap way to get a sale regardless of the situation. Typically, an under sell is when a rep actually sells less than necessary or what is required by a customer. In their anxiousness to get a sale, some reps will offer a solution that, while low in price, does not meet a customer's needs.

The long and the short of the under-sell is simply this: The customer does not get value in the long run. Sooner or later, he or she will wake up to the fact that the item purchased is inadequate for their needs. This may lead to a complaint and certainly will minimize any opportunity for future sales. As for the reps, apart from doing their company a disservice, they are shortchanging themselves. In short, it is a lose-lose-lose situation.

I mention this because some reps will use the down-sell to justify an under sell. They'll take the strategy and employee it in their regular selling process. So, let me repeat, a down-sell comes at the end of a call. It is a back-up strategy that is held in reserve and is used only when legitimately applicable.

The Four-Step Down-Sell System

Have I mentioned that the down-sell comes at the end of the call? Oh yeah, I did. Okay, this means that you have listened to your customer and prospect and you have heard the balk at your price and/or recommendations or they wish to cancel an order or subscription. Moving from this point, here are the four steps.

Step 1: Listen, Question and Listen

The first step is to listen to the customer or prospect. Listen to their objection, their concerns, the reason or explanation of why they can't buy or why they are cancelling. Sometimes, it's easy. They'll tell you straight away without any prompting.

If they don't fess up, or if they're unclear in their explanation, you need to question it so that you precisely understand the situation. There are a couple of specific techniques you can use.

The Explain Technique. The "explain technique" is great for cancellations.   It is a simple, open-ended question that looks something like this:

> **"Mr. Potter, could you explain to me why**
> **you are cancelling?"**

Watch your tone. Be sincere, otherwise it might sound a bit abrasive. The customer tends to get a little defensive if they are caught off guard. After you ask the question, SHUT UP. You may have seen me state this tip before. Silence is a powerful ally on the phone.

Then you need to listen to the response. Is the cancellation because the product no longer has value or was there a problem? These are two different scenarios. If you can solve the problem, you may not have to down-sell at all. If the issue is with value, a down-sell might fit.

We saw this with Patrick Hennessy in Australia. Patrick works for a company that sells summaries of business books. The offer is bundled, which means a subscriber gets executive book summaries on both leadership AND sales and marketing. Over time, it was discovered that many subscribers were cancelling because one of the topics did not really apply to them. For instance, sales and marketing executives were not interested in leadership,

while CEOs were not always interested in sales and marketing.

The "explain technique" helps reveal this. Once Hennessy
understood the reason for the cancellation, he was in a
position to offer the down-sell. He could offer the subscriber a lower priced packet that covered only sales and
marketing or only leadership. The end result was that the
customer got what he/she wanted and the book company
managed to keep the customer, albeit it at a lower price…
but better than no customer at all.

The Expectation Technique. The "expectation technique"
works very well when you encounter a customer who has
experienced sticker shock. It looks like this:

> **"Can I ask you, Ms. Granger, what did you
> expect to pay?"**

The technique is designed to get the customer to state
their expectation in terms of budget. As Greg Gilbert at
Affymetrix discovered, universities and colleges operate
under strict budgets. Their ability to dig deeper is not a
simple task. Once Gilbert understands the budget range,
he can scan products that are relative to the customer's
needs, and, if applicable, offer an alternative.

Step 2: The Bridge
By now you should be entirely familiar with the bridge.
The bridge alerts the customer or prospect that you are
shifting gears. It gets them to listen. The bridge in the
down-sell looks like this:

> **"Based on what you have told me, here's
> what I would like to recommend…"**

> **"I understand your situation. Here's an al-
> ternative…"**

> **"I have an idea that might benefit you..."**

> **"Here's a suggestion that just might fit..."**

Every one of these bridge statements acts as a pre-text to your recommendation. In effect, they alter or prepare your client for the next step.

Step 3: Present the Offer and the Benefit
The add-on selling system for the down-sell is no different from any other add-on application at this stage. You present your offer or recommendation and you provide a benefit.

> **"Mr. Potter, based on what you have told me, I would like to recommend our Sales and Marketing Executive Book Summary. This is a scaled down version of what you're currently receiving. It will give you all the sales and marketing summaries without the leadership summaries. This will allow you to stay focused and read only those summaries that apply to your area of expertise. This package comes at a price of only $99.00/year which is a savings of $56.00 from your current subscription."**

As you can see, the offer is relatively short and sweet. The down-sell focuses on a product that is lower in price but more targeted to the customer's needs. Here's another look.

> **"Ms. Granger, given your budget, here's a suggestion that just might fit. We have a flow meter unit called The 110. Call it a "mid-size" version of the 120. It carefully measures the flow of fluid, but unlike the 120 it is analog and not digital. The reporting tape is not quite as extensive, but given what you have told me about your key**

> parameters, the 110 covers them all. In short
> you can have all the critical benefits of the 120
> but at a budget you can afford."

In certain cancellation situations, you might want to save
the sale simply by cutting the price with no change to the
product. For instance, the offer might look like this:

> "Mr. Weasley, I see that you have been a cus-
> tomer for the last 3 years and we would truly
> hate to lose you. Suppose I could offer you
> the newsletter at $150.00 instead of the usual
> rate of $179.00. That is just about a $30
> savings."

Step 4: The Close
The close brings closure to the down-sell. You need to initiate some sort of a close so that the customer can respond.

> "How does that sound?"

> "Can I sign you up for the marketing and
> sales version?"

> "Would you like to proceed?"

> "How does that look to you?"

> "Do you think that might benefit you?"

> "Can I use the same credit card we have on
> file?"

> "Shall we get started?"

There are dozens of ways to close the sale. Choose one and
use it. Closing reduces the call length. It either gets the

sale (or saves the sale) or it doesn't. Either way, there's no guessing and messing around.

The Add-On To the Down-Sell

Okay, just to muddy the waters a little more, once you down-sell you can actually implement another add-on sell.

Down-Selling lends itself to add-on selling!

Think about it. You have just been down-sold. You dodged a bullet and it saved you the sale. The customer is happy. He got a better price, or he got a product that met his needs. And because the customer is pleased, the reciprocity factor kicks in. Remember that? Your down-sell creates a feeling of reciprocity in many customers (i.e., the need to repay you for your efforts). The time to add-on sell kicks in again.

The Cross-Sell

I saw this with Jason at Oak Bay Marina. I actually booked there last year and selected a fishing package. I was one of those customers who suffered from sticker shock. I didn't realize the price for bagging a few salmon for my kids and myself was so…well, steep. But there was another issue swimming around in my mind. My wife. While we boys are off playing (fishing) what was she to do? So, I just couldn't justify it.

Jason down-sold me AFTER he asked me to explain why I had backed off. The down-sell was to say that we did not have to book a salmon tour at all, and that we could simply relax in our cottage on the mountain shore. He tallied up the price and I was happy.

Here's what happened next.

> **"Jim, while I have you, you mentioned a couple of things earlier. First, you really**

> **wanted to relax in a quiet area and you also
> though your wife might like to go whale watch-
> ing or on an eco tour, right? Here's an idea you
> might like. We have a cottage set off about a
> quarter of a mile from the main lodge. No
> neighbors. Nestled in the firs. Four bed-
> rooms. Four baths. And an outdoor hot tub.
> It might be something to consider. Bev
> might like it. It's only $49.00 more per
> night."**

Oh, those magic words. Quiet, luxurious and my wife
would think I was a hero. I said to myself, "Hey, what the
heck, I just saved a pile by not taking the fishing package,
so why not?" See how the mind works? I perceived I had
saved by being sold. In my mind, I had more income to
blow elsewhere. And I did. I really looked like a hero.
Really! Jason continued:

> **"I mentioned an eco tour. I think you will
> love this. We have half-day packages where
> you go out to the ocean and we take you key
> ecological areas where you'll see bald eagles,
> Orcas, unbelievable scenery, tidal pools,
> seals and bears."**

The bears did it. If I were a hero for the secluded cottage
selection, then I would be a god for the bears. I was. At
least for a little while. Kidding aside, we saw three bears.

Alrighty then. Here's what happened. When I tallied the
add-on sales made by Jason, we were just a tad under the
amount he had originally quoted. His down-sell saved the
sale and his cross-sells brought the dollar amount right
back up.

The Referral
Just to give you another example, at Clement Communications poster programs and newsletter subscriptions are
cancelled from time to time. Attempts are made to save

the sale by questioning the client but it doesn't always work out. But there is still an opportunity to squeeze or leverage the moment by asking for a referral. There are two ways that Clement can do this:

The Internal Referral. Here is one way they ask for a referral.

> **"Mr. Bauer, before we conclude, I wonder if you can give me the name of anyone else in your company that might be interested in a communications program? For instance, a quality or security manager?"**

Calling to cancel an order is not something most people like to do because it is a little awkward. If you are polite and courteous in how you handle the matter, the customer tends to feel relieved and is more prone to give back by providing you with a name.

Internal referrals work very well because the prospect has a direct affinity with the person who gave the referral. *The External Referral.* The external referral asks for a referral outside the company. It looks like this:

> **"Ms. Drill, before we conclude, who do you know who might benefit from a poster program such as this?"**

The two referrals are really one and the same. Either way it is a chance to salvage what you can from a cancellation. Who knows what if might bring?

Summary

The down-sell is your back-up, reserve offer. Having a down-sell offer prepared ahead of time can save you countless customers and countless dollars.

Chapter17

The Follow-Up Call

Do you want to get the best results possible with your add-on application? Do you want to be the leader of the pack?

Regardless of whether you are in sales or service, or whether you are a manager or a rep, the easiest way to increase the odds of success is to make a follow-up call to your external and internal customers. The follow-up call reminds, prompts, prods or gently pushes the customer to take action. Don't get me wrong, not all applications and not all customers need a follow-up call, but some do. Some customers and some applications scream for a follow call or visit.

This chapter is about making a follow-up contact to increase the odds of success.

Follow-Up Defined

A follow-up call is nothing more than a call or visit to either an external or internal customer (see below) to ensure that the add-on sell gets acted upon. It is reminder. It is a checkup. It is a feedback loop. A prompt. A catalyst. Call it what you like, but it is a means of ensuring greater success.

The benefits of a follow-up phone call are enticing. You should know them because they'll compel you to pick up the phone and dial.

Higher Conversion Rate

First and foremost, a follow-up call creates a higher conversion rate. It makes perfect sense. A call acts as a prompt or reminder for those clients who have not taken action. I am not implying that all add-on applications require a follow-up. We'll look at that below. For the moment, I am saying that when you do make a follow-up call, the conversion rate is higher. How much higher will depend on a number of circumstances but trust me (and any experienced sales person) when I say a follow-up means greater success.

Status Gauge

A follow-up call gives you the status of an account or a sale or a lead. It is information. Sometimes leads are sent by customer service to sales. A follow-up call determines the status of those leads. It keeps the sale's wheel greased because, as we all know, the squeaky wheel gets the oil

Feedback Loop

Not only does a follow-up call give you the status of a particular situation, it can also provide constructive feedback. For instance, let's say you send 10 leads to the sales department and not a single lead converts. Luck? Chance? A poor lead? Poor follow-up by sales? Who's to say until you have taken the time and effort to find out. Maybe you have to change the way you qualify a lead before sending it or maybe the sales team is not following up until weeks later. The follow-up call, if used correctly, can give you all sorts of feedback that can help hone skills, techniques and strategies which can give you better results.

Customer Service Par Excellence

A follow-up call to a customer who had a complaint or problem or a customer service issue can go a long way to mend fences. It creates a favorable impression in the mind of the customer: *"Hey, a company that cares!"* It builds a relationship. Every time you make a positive impression with your customer, good things can happen. It could mean more repeat business. It could mean leads and re-ferrals. You get the picture.

More Sales

Every contact with a client is another opportunity to use your add-on selling techniques. If you've solved the cus-tomer's problem on the Help Desk, and you make a follow-up call, there is a possible cross-sell opportunity. A call to assess the effectiveness of a service call is another possible selling opportunity.

The Two Customers

There are two customers who can benefit from the follow-up call: External and internal customers. Let's look at each.

1. The External Customer

This one is easy. The external customers are those cus-tomers who actually purchase from you. People who use your services. The end-user. They pay your company and indirectly, they pay your salary or commission or bonus. So they're important, right? As we have learned, the more they take advantage of your offers, the more satisfied they are and the more satisfied you and your company are. Simple logic. The follow-up calls help convert more sales and keep everyone happy.

First things first. Not every customer needs a follow-up call and not every add-on application requires a follow-up. It is not always practical nor time and cost-effective. But, there are some applications where a follow-up call makes perfect sense.

Complaints. A follow-up call to a customer who has had a complaint can do wonders at keeping the customer and getting him/her to buy more. Customers love it. Who wouldn't? Here is a company and an individual who is taking the time to do a little extra, to gauge their satisfaction level. It is such a rare kind of call that it will amaze and delight the client.

Why would you do this? Apart from the goodwill you create, a follow-up call gives you an opportunity to do add-on selling. Think about it. Assuming the customer is now satisfied, you can cross-sell, generate a lead, get a referral or gather market intelligence.

Market Intelligence. Personally, I have received dozens of telephone market surveys, both formal and informal. I have absolutely no idea whatever became of the information I provided. No big deal, right? Wrong, bucko! The fall out has been that I don't bother to provide feedback to any vendor if they ask. The "take, take, take" mentality of vendors has soured my disposition. The good information I have remains locked away. I don't think I am alone.

Every now and then, a follow-up call to a customer who has given you market intelligence, feedback, ideas or suggestions is a great idea. You'll shock 'em dead. Not only is it a chance to say thank you and garner additional information, it too is a chance to add-on sell. (NOTE: I am not saying you SHOULD add-on sell with every call back. That can get a little too self serving. I am simply saying there is an opportunity, *if appropriate*, to do so.)

Service/Help Desk. A follow-up call made to a customer who has recently had service or has received assistance from a Help Desk isn't a bad idea. First of all, it would delight the average customer and secondly, it opens up the opportunity for any number of add-on applications. And thirdly, lest we forget, a follow-up call can be used to assess the effectiveness of the service or help desk rep. It can be used to help identify if there is a problem or it can be used as a way to recognize the superior service.

You might not make a follow-up call to all customers. Perhaps it is only a small percentage. Perhaps it is only to those who have called on certain problems or concerns. Perhaps you do a blitz or maybe it is ongoing. The real point is this: there is value in the call.

Lead Generation. Calling back customers who have provided you a lead is a novel idea. It helps you determine the status of the lead. There is more on this particular topic in the next section. Read it. It's important because it is almost always a surefire way to inject sales into your company immediately.

2. The Internal Customer

The second type of customer is a little more subtle and a little more complex. They are the internal customers. These are the other departments you work with. The ones who might be integral to the success of your sale. They might be sales, marketing, research, operations…any of whom could play an integral role in the add-on selling program.

Three Reasons to Make the Internal Follow-up

- **To Ensure That Action Has Occurred.** First, to ensure that the lead, information, referral, tip, complaint…whatever…has been followed up by the appropriate department. Your add-on selling program cannot work in a vacuum on its own, otherwise, it will be short-lived. And inasmuch as a department might agree to cooperate with you in *theory*, the *practice* might be a different story. Let's face it, other departments have their responsibilities, concerns, demands, etc. If you pass a lead or a referral or a tidbit of market intelligence, there is a chance it can get lost in the shuffle, forgotten, misplaced, or ignored. By making a follow-up call to these internal departments, you increased the likelihood of action being taken. Your call acts as a gentle (or sometimes, not so gentle) prompt or reminder.

- **To Measure and Assess.** Getting the status is a little more different than prompting. By status, I am referring to the process of gathering data on what happened with the referral, lead, etc. The data you collect allows you to measure and assess. Information is power. By collecting data, you can identify trends, look for opportunities, build case studies, and ultimately measure success. Assessing how you or your department has done, helps you determine if the add-on program is working or not. This is vital for all those who look at your time and effort and demand it if it's worthwhile.

- **To Get Feedback.** By feedback, I mean talking one-to-one with individuals who get your leads, referrals, market intelligence, and so forth. By feedback, I mean making a follow-up call and asking the individual what is working and what is not. Suppose you measure and assess your lead generation program and you discover that not a single lead has been converted. Yikes! Is it the rep generating the lead? Is it the kind of questions you are asking? It could be any number of things. Feedback in a more qualitative dialogue that helps you adjust your tactics.

There are some add-on selling applications where an internal call is a good idea. The first one, lead generation, is perhaps the most significant. Be brave of heart when you read it because it touches on a sensitive issue.

Lead Generation. Here is a vitally important application for a follow-up call.

When a lead is generated and passed on to another department–inside or field sales–a follow-up call should be made to that customer by the department that generated the lead. So, in other words, if the customer service department generated a lead and passed it on to field sales, the customer service department should follow-up with the customer about four or five days later.

The purpose of the call is twofold. First, it is made as a service call to ensure satisfaction. Second, and more significantly, it is made to ensure that the field rep has made some sort of contact on the lead.

Right about this time, field reps and others accused me of checking up on them. Spying. Prying. Butting in. I used to deny it. I used to come up with all sorts of reasons clad in the thin disguise of a customer service call. But then, I simply gave up.

If it looks like I am suggesting a follow-up program that checks up on the sales department, I am.

Let me repeat that so it is clear to everyone reading this: I AM SAYING YOU SHOULD CHECK UP ON YOUR SALES DEPARTMENT.

That won't make me popular. But almost 20 years of consulting and developing lead generation strategies have shown me one thing consistently, time after time: lead follow-up by sales reps is poor. Maybe not in your company but with the dozens and dozens of companies I have worked with, I have seen an alarming majority of leads simply forgotten or ignored.

I understand why. Leads mean work. If the leads are poor, it means lots of work and lots of wasted time. Sales reps complain that they get poor leads from Help Desks, Customer Service Departments and the like. "Once burned, twice cautious" is the cry. Fair enough. This is why communication between sales and other departments is vital. It should be an ongoing process whereby sales reps can feedback to other departments and help educate and train them on more effective means of generating leads or referrals.

Even so, there is sales resistance. I am not precisely sure why this is so. Perhaps it is ego. But, I do know that when we implemented a lead follow-up program with a property and casualty insurance company, the lead conversion rate went from 2.5% to 38%. Here's what happened.

Leads were generated from inbound calls taken by customer service reps. The leads were sent to field sales and a paltry conversion rate of 2.5% was achieved. Something seemed wrong to me. We had good information because we had some great qualifying questions. So, I implemented a follow-up call campaign. The field reps were given two business days to make contact with the prospect. It did not mean that they had to visit them, it simply meant a live contact would be made. To ensure this would happen, a follow-up call would be made by the customer service rep to the customer one day after that.

The sales reps screamed bloody murder. They were outraged. How dare we check up on them! What about integrity?

Whatever...

Within three weeks, sales were converting at 38%. The average value of the sale was $2,000. The reps received commissions from each sale.

You see, it is human nature to procrastinate on a lead given to us by someone who may not have the same job profile as us. It is human nature to procrastinate when it interrupts OUR plan and approach to the market. I understand these things and you should too. But, the results speak for themselves.

Market Intelligence. An internal follow-up call to your internal clients in marketing makes a good deal of sense, too. Is the effort made by you and/or your sales reps worth the time? Is the information that is gathered being used or simply discarded? Everyone likes to feel that they are contributing. If there is no feedback or if the efforts are simply not creating results, it becomes difficult to maintain an add-on program.

The Five-Step Process for Follow-Up
Most add-on selling applications use the Four-Step System. I am assuming right now that any follow-up is made by telephone. (Of course, a visit or an e-mail will work as a follow-up technique, but let's focus on the telephone.) The follow-up has five basic steps.

Step 1: Your Full Name
It should be obvious, but bears mention nonetheless. You state your FULL name for two reasons. First of all, the very first question anyone asks when the phone rings is who is calling. Tell them. Secondly, using your FULL names give you a certain degree of status at a subconscious level, compared to simply using your first name only. First names tend to conjure up images of a low-level clerk. Not fair. I know that. At the end of the day, it is your choice, but sales is made up of dozens of little things done right. There is, of course, an exception. If you are calling your buddy Felix in the sales department and you've know him for years, you can use your first name only.

Step 2: State Your Company/Department Name
This, too, is obvious but worth the space on which it is typed. Stating your company name or your department gives the listener a quick reference point.

Step 3: Bridge

This is important. Unexpected telephone calls are intrusions to most people. They don't sit around and hope that someone out of the blue will give them a call. Consequently, it is vital that you cut to the quick and tell the listener why you are calling. It is professional, time effective and appreciated.

As noted author and sales trainer Art Sobczak points out, "Your follow-up call should serve to smoothly bring the customer's state-of-mind back to the point where it was when you ended the previous conversation." This is called the "bridge".

Step 4: Ask

Typically, you are making a follow-up call to ask the status of a situation or gather feedback or confirm. Do that. Don't beat around the bush. Here are a few examples of Steps 3 and 4 put together:

Follow-up Call to a External Customer – lead generation

> **"Wendi, I am calling to resume our conversation last week when we discussed the possibility of you signing up on our corporate account program, which would reduce the hassle of over the border shipping. Have you had a chance to speak to one of our inside sales reps?"**

Follow-up Call – Service Rep to Customer

> **"Mr. Davison, the reason for my call is a follow-up on our discussion on Tuesday about using high-speed Internet and networking your computers to give you greater produc-**

tivity. You mentioned you were going to
speak with your partner to determine the
next steps. Have you had an opportunity to
review it with him?"

Follow-up Call – Internal Customer – Lead Status

"Pat, I am following up on the lead I sent
you on Thursday concerning Brian Jeffrey
and his interest in compensation consulting.
Have you spoken with Brian?"

Follow-up Call – Complaint

"Ms. O'Brien, The reason for my call is simply to follow-up the call you made to us on
the 15th regarding the error on your account.
I wanted to make sure that the error has
been cleared up and ask if there is anything
else I can do. How have things progressed?

Step 5: Close

The final step is to close the call. Naturally, you might
have a dialogue of some length with the customer. You
may have to investigate further or solve another problem.
But, at some point, the call will need to be terminated.
You have two choices.

The first choice is a simple "thank you" and "good bye".
Many of your calls will be that easy.

The second choice is an add-on sell. You have to be sharp
here. You also have to be diplomatic. If the customer is
pleased and receptive and if there is a legitimate opportu-

nity, you can use the moment for an add-on sell. If so, go
back to the Four-Step Process and go for it!

Pre-Call Planning

An outbound follow-up call is a proactive event. This
means you initiate it and, ultimately, you control it.
This gives you the advantage. The advantage is that you
can plan it before you pick up the phone.

Pre-call planning does not take a long time, but the few seconds you take to think out your strategy can spell the difference between a professional call and a mediocre call.
The sad truth is that many reps simply pick up the phone
and speak from the cuff. Many times, the calls is simple
enough for this to be effective. But, there are some calls,
follow-ups on complaints, for instance, that would benefit
from a few moments of thought.

Here's how you pre-call plan:

First, grab a sheet of paper. You are going to create a
roadmap of your outbound call.

Write out your primary objective: what is it precisely that
you want to achieve? What is the most important thing
you want to happen

Next, list your secondary objectives. This is a great opportunity to think about any add-on selling applications that
might fit. Can you get a referral? Is there a possible cross-
sell that fits this scenario? Is there a lead that might be
lurking in the weeds?

The next step is to script out your opening statement with
particular emphasis on Steps 3 and 4. The smoother you
sound, the more professional you sound. The more professional you sound, the more successful your call will be.

List any other questions you might need to ask (there might be more than one). Writing them down ensures you will remember to ask.

Leave space on your sheet for notes. Listen with a pen in hand. Don't rely on your memory. There might be some action you'll have to take. For example, maybe the customer needs you to fax something. Jot it down so you won't forget. They might give you a referral, so make sure you get the name, number, etc.

The pre-call planning sheet is what separates highly effective customer service, help desk, sales reps and others from highly mediocre customer service, help desk, sales reps and others. Use it.

Summary
The follow-up is not something that should be used all the time. It is another tool in your add-on selling toolbox. You use it when you need it. You use it when it applies. And, when you do use it, use it properly to get maximum results.

Chapter 18

Job Aids: Making Add-On Selling Easier And Faster

In this chapter you will find information on how to create job aids that will make add-on selling easier. This chapter is ideal for anyone who uses add-on techniques, but it is particularly helpful for sales supervisors and managers who are trying to implement an add-on program with their sales team.

What's a Job Aid?

A job aid is a tool that makes the add-on selling process that much easier. By a tool, I mean anything from a script, to a selling chart, to a pop-up menu, to a "Frequently Asked Questions" grid. Virtually, anything that helps prompt or assist in the add-on selling process.

Why should you use a job aid? You can look at this one from several angles:

The Sales Rep. If you are a sales rep, job aids helps make the add-on selling easier in several ways:

- they can help remind you to add-on sell with every call.

- they can make the transition to the add-on smoother and more professional.

- they can help you eliminate fumbling about for the right words and the right offer.

- they can speed up the process and the call length collectively.

- job aids help you sell more in less time.

The Supervisor/Manager. If you are a supervisor or a manager, a job is a must. Period.

- Job aids ensure that everyone in your department or on your team is "singing from the same hymn book." This means quality control,

- they are great training tools; they speed up the learning process, and,

- job aids make monitoring and coaching easier and this saves you time.

Types of Job Aids

The following is a list of some of the more common job aids. Your job is to analyze your situation and determine which job aids will be best for you. Take the time and create the job aids. I kid you not, they make a significant difference in sales results.

Scripts

Okay, let's deal with this sensitive topic once and for all. I talked about scripts in an earlier chapter, but it is important to reference it again. Mention the word "script" to sales reps and watch them curl their lips in disgust. Scripts conjure up images of monotone, lifeless recitals of offers.

First, let's get something straight. When you boil it down, scripts themselves are not what we dislike, but rather a poorly delivered script. Actors and actresses deliver scripts in movies that make us laugh, cry, get angry, feel pain and anxiety. Every one of them reads from a script. But they read it well.

Just to clarify further, when I talk about scripts, I am not talking about scripting the entire call *from beginning to end.* I am simply talking about scripting **certain key parts** of your dialogue or offer. If there are 20 or 30 reps in your call center who make or take fifty or sixty (or whatever) calls in a day, and all of them will be offering a cross-sell on a certain item, why would you not have a small "script" to describe the offer?

The alternative is to have all your reps improvising the offer with every single call. That'll kill quality control. You'll get scattered results. But the real irony is that, typically, your reps begin to develop their own script after a period of time (whether they realize it or not) because they find it easier. This is great, provided that their scripted phrase/offer/suggestion/reply is good and consistent.

Whether you want to admit it or not, scripts work exceedingly well when well-delivered. Scripting certain key parts to your add-on and delivering them well will make a significant difference in your selling efforts.

Call Guides

Call guides are sort of like scripts, but I tend to think of them as road maps or "call maps". Call guides direct the flow of questions depending on answers, and they are particularly effective if you are doing some basic qualification.

For example, one of the absolute best call guide/scripts I have ever heard or seen comes from The Wine Shippers in

Chicago. The Wine Shippers is a U.S.-wide, direct-to-consumer wine merchant. Instead of buying wine at a retail outlet, you buy it direct by telephone from a broker.

Roger Long is one of the top merchants at Wine Shippers. We did a little role play together on the telephone. I was the customer and Roger was making an outbound call to me. I did not know it at the time, but he was using a call guide with certain scripted parts to sell me about some wine. I will not go into all the details. What is important to note is how Roger used the call guide (the lines that point you to answers) and certain scripted parts to gather information and move the client (me) towards a decision.

"Mr. Domanski this is Roger Long from Wine Shippers. Jim, your name was passed along to me recently as a person who enjoys a fine glass of wine from time to time. Is that correct?"

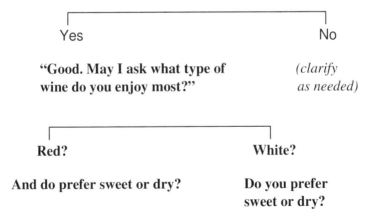

Yes   No

"Good. May I ask what type of   *(clarify*
wine do you enjoy most?"   *as needed)*

Red?   White?

And do prefer sweet or dry?   **Do you prefer**
                                                          sweet or dry?

"That's great. The Wine Shippers selects certain European as well as California wines for exclusive handling in the United States. Since we market these wines by telephone, we don't have the fancy overhead of a normal wine store; therefore, saving our clients money anywhere from 25%-30%. Of course, what this means is significant savings on your favorite wines."

"Jim, you said that you enjoy a dry red, am I correct?"

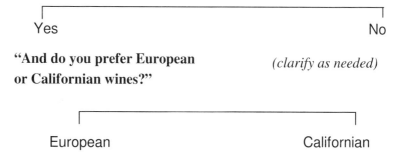

Yes — "And do you prefer European or Californian wines?"

No — *(clarify as needed)*

European / Californian

"Great, in that case I have something that might interest you?"

(Refer to European Wine Detail Flip Chart) *(Refer to Californian Wine Detail Flip Chart)*

Call guides like these have been around for years. But, this does not diminish their worth or value in managing a call. As I mentioned, they act as a road map to a destination. After a while, you'll get to know the roads well and the "map" is not necessary. The same thing applies to calls: after a while, you will know your way around and the guide will only be used as a quick reference.

And here's the point: call guides are great learning tools. Call guides are great reference tools. Use them for those purposes.

Incidentally, Roger went on in a similar manner until I was quite ready to buy, even though we were doing a role play. (Too bad I live in Canada -- can't get the wines shipped up here.)

You can see that the above call guide uses lines to guide the rep based on the answer to particular question. It can be a simple or a complex schematic. Either way, it is meant to guide the rep quickly through a series of questions. The real benefit is that it helps take the thinking of the right question out of the equation. The rep can concentrate on the answers.

I like to put call guides on colored sheets, laminate them and post them on the cubicle. Kind of reminds me of the things my kids would create in kindergarten. Who cares? They work.

Add-On Chart

An "add-on chart" is simply a quick reference chart that lists a product or a service that a client might typically order. Besides, it is an add-on product or service that might complement the purchase. You can fancy it up by adding a benefit. For example:

PRODUCT/ SERVICE	ADD-ON	BENEFIT
Deluxe fishing vacation package	Whale-watching tour	Greater enjoyment
	Golf tee times	Avoid disappointment

This chart is for cross-selling. You can create a similar one for up-selling. You can do whatever you want. In essence, the chart is a more detailed form of a call guide except it relates directly to an offer.

These things are great. Don't quibble. Create them and use them.

FAQ Charts

"FAQ" stands for "Frequently Asked Questions". You can and should create these charts when you anticipate questions regarding your add-on. For example, you might create a chart for whale watching questions. Questions that spring to my mind are: How much does it cost? How often do they run? In what kind of boat? How long are they? How often do you see whales? What kind of whales?

Brainstorm together as a group and develop some answers. The more questions you can answer, the more likely the customer will sign on. You help reduce or eliminate the stall because you have the answers handy.

Interestingly, a good number of companies ignore this one. It's a shame because it really is a no-brainer. Pretend you are the customer listening to the offer. What would you typically ask? Be proactive. Have the replies listed for the sake of the customer and the sake of the rep.

Objections Charts

Objections charts are really another form of an FAQ chart. Essentially, you list the anticipated objections on the left hand side and your replies on the right.

The only trouble with an objections chart is that what customers say isn't always what they mean. The best way to handle an objection is to question the customer to determine the real objection.

But in saying this, you must remember that an add-on sale should be relatively quick and easy to understand. The client should not have to do a great deal of thinking. In other words, it should not be so complex that you are into a whole new selling cycle. That's not the point. This is why "frequently asked questions" tend to be a better way of labeling an objection because it implies that the questions are sincere, whereas an objection can have an ulterior motive.

"FAB"

Talk about sales 101. FAB stands for "feature", "advantage", and "benefit". I won't go into detail on these three elements. That should be basic for anyone in sales. Suffice it to say, a FAB chart helps describe a product or a service in clear, benefit-oriented terms.

Suppose you are a rep at Franklin Covey and you wish to cross-sell a storage binder for the Monarch Time System. Here's what the FAB Chart might look like:

FEATURE	ADVANTAGE	BENEFIT
3-ring binder	can store two year's worth of documents	saves you time searching for documents

A FAB chart is not remarkably different than an add-on chart. The add-on chart describes the full offer, whereas the FAB chart can break the offer into component parts. If you want, you could use this chart to describe your full offer.

In any event, it is a means of communicating a message more effectively.

Product Description Flip Charts
The Wine Shippers have flip charts describing the wines being offered. A FAB chart is not necessary for something like this. A FAB sheet is not necessary for someone buying a scarf and who has a catalog in front of her. However, what is handy to have is a brief description of key products or offers. Perhaps one or two lines. How about this for a European Pinot Noir:

> **"...slightly impetuous but eminently palletable...exciting and enticing as the French Quarter, but as mellow and gentle as a minuet by Mozart..."**

Okay, a bit pretentious. But, I can guarantee the wine snobs will love it. Stick that on a product description flip chart and watch the crates go out the door.

Catalog, Brochures, Flyers and Web Sites
One of the best tools for cross-selling and up-selling is your company's product brochures or catalogs.

Lori Albright, supervisor at Victoria's Secret, has her reps use the catalog to cross-sell on a regular basis. They do an awesome job. I know. I have experienced it. When I order a product, the rep will suggest a cross-sell to compliment the items by saying something like,

> **"You know Mr. Domanski, a matching scarf would really compliment the sweater you just bought for your wife. If you take a look**

> **on page 28, you can see a perfect match on the upper left corner. See how it highlights the blue in the sweater. Your wife would love it."**

The visual image that a catalog or brochure produces is powerful.

IBM uses their website in a similar manner. When the IBM rep begins to chat with a prospect, he or she will have the prospect move throughout the web site to show how certain items might give the ThinkPad more power or extra features.

Franklin Covey's website uses star bursts to remind clients of additional products when they are browsing and ordering online. No reps are involved at this stage, so it is subtle, but every effective.

Automated or Manual?

I get this question a hundred times in a year: what is better, a manual or an automated job aid?

First let's define what we mean. A manual job aid is something you create on paper. It sits on a desk, in a binder or on a cubicle wall. An automated job is one that is created on the computer. It is stored digitally.

Here's my two cents worth based on ten years of observation.

Automated Job Aids

Automated systems are great if you can make them work. At Computer Software Upgrades, a rather gifted computer guy was able to manipulate the ACT! software so that when reps enter certain product codes, a pop-up menu appeared on the screen with a scripted offer that applied to the particular product. It was awesome. Fast, effective, and successful.

But, here's the catch. In ten years of consulting and training, this has been the *only* example I have seen where an automated job aid has worked so effectively. What I have seen is valiant attempts to automate with mediocre results. Here are the problems as I have seen them.

- Automating job aids takes a lot of time, effort and expertise. It's a chore. A real pain.

- Automated systems tend to be expensive. You need techie people to create, implement, fix, change and maintain the program.

- Generally speaking, automated systems lack the flexibility to change quickly. It seems that by the time the job aid was up and ready to go, the opportunity had passed or changed.

- The next thing I have observed is that automated job aids are somewhat complex and cumbersome to work with. A typical example is seeing reps frantically hot-keying between two systems (the order system and the inventory). This simply serves to increase the call length and decrease the customer's patience. Not worth it in my books.

Inevitably, I have watched automated systems crash, and the whole add-on process come to a screeching halt.

Having said all that, I will admit that I am not a technical sort. Heck, maybe there dozens of great systems out there and I have simply not seen them. If you have a system or process for automated job aids, like Computer Software Upgrades, one which is fast and easy and affordable to implement, then I would love to hear from you.

Manual Systems

Gee, guess what I am going to say about manual systems. I like them. At least I like them better than the automated approach.

I like them because they are comparatively faster and easier to implement and use. The operative word is USE. When you use a job aid, you get results.

I like manual job aids because they are simple and because they can be changed almost instantly. If you find a script, a chart or an offer is not working effectively, you can bang out a new job aid in no time flat and begin using it. It is adjustable and dynamic.

They're dirt cheap. You don't need your 14-year-old computer-wizard or a grad student at MIT to program every single change. I can do it… and that says a lot.

The drawbacks? Well, there are some. Manual (paper) systems can be cumbersome if you have multiple offers for multiple products. In fact, it is sometimes impossible to manage. I have seen binders crammed full of job aids, and the poor reps have to leaf through page after page. Not a pretty sight.

They can create clutter, get mangled, or get lost in the shuffle. Not pretty either.

The Solution

If you have the resources, the time and the expertise, use the automated system. If you don't, use the manual system. Whatever you choose, use job aids because they work.

Making Job Aids User-Friendly

The following quick tips generally apply to manual sys-Tems, but they can work with an automated system.

- **Use 14 point or 16 point typeface.** It is easier to read (easier to read means easier to use. Easier to use means sales results)

- Use serif font, like this one (as opposed to sans serif like this stuff here because it is harder to read).

- DON'T USE CAPS (THIS GETS HARD ON YOUR EYES).

- Use different colored sheets for your add-on and FAB charts, FAQ, etc. This can apply to automated systems as well.

- Laminate the sheets so they last longer.

- Post the job aid in places where they will get read and used.

- If you have a call guide, place them on huge 11 x 17 sheets so you can draw lots of lines and directions. Tape a couple of them together. They're big and bulky and they work.

- Use color codes. "Yes" answers are in blue; "no" answers are in red.

- Create the job aids together as a team. More buy-in means better results

- Use binders with colorful tabs to delineate products or offers.

- Review every new job aid thoroughly. Role play using them.

- Change and edit the job aid when necessary.

- Date the job aids in the lower left or right-hand corner to ensure the right job aids are being used.

- Collect, toss or destroy old job aids (get rid of the clutter and manage the paper).

Summary

I find I can garden better with a rake or a hoe. I can remove the snow better with a shovel. Tools. You can add-on sell more effectively using tools like those mentioned here. Create the job aids and sell like crazy.

Chapter 19

The Dark Side: How to Avoid The Misuse and Abuse of Add-On Selling

Did you know that George Lucas, the brilliant creator of the Star Wars movies, once gave an interview regarding add-on selling?

Yes, it's true. One of the key themes of the movie was the use of the "Force" which was some sort of metaphysical/spiritual strength or power within the universe that, with training, could be captured and harnessed. If you recall the movies, you will know that there was a good side of the Force, employed by Jedi Knights like Luke Skywalker, Obi-Wan Kenobi and Qui-Gon Jin. You will also know there was a dark side of the Force, employed by evil Siths like Darth Vader, Darth Maul, and Emperor Palpatine.

Lucas pointed out that add-on selling is like the "Force". When used well, it can harness untold sales and glory, but when used poorly, add-on selling can wreak horror throughout the sales universe.

Just kidding.

I made up the part about the interview.

As far as I know, Lucas never gave such an interview. Apart from being a clever way to get your attention, it does serve as an excellent metaphor to illustrate the two sides of add-on selling. Add-on selling has a very good side but there is also an evil side to it. Like Jedi Knights, sales reps can be lured to the dark side of selling.

In this chapter, we'll come clean with the dark side of add-on selling. We'll look at how you can avoid the misuse and abuse of add-on selling that sometimes tempts the user. Poor, inconsistent, or unethical use of this technique can bring about the ruin of the program and so much more.

We touched on the dark side earlier in the book. We mentioned some of things that clients do not like. But in this chapter, we will focus on this issue a little more closely.

This small but important chapter examines the ethics of add-on selling. It will look at what you should avoid and what you should NOT do when using this powerful technique. This chapter will look at how to avoid the "Dark Side of Add-On Selling".

Understanding the Dark Side

I'll be straight with you. Some of your customers or prospects won't appreciate your add-on efforts. There are some clients who are cynical, jaded and leery. Some might even be downright nasty.

The explanation for this comes from Jason Guille, a tele-sales rep at Oak Bay Marine Group in Victoria, British Columbia. Oak Bay sells vacation packages for avid fishermen and Jason, to me, is one of the best of the best when it comes to tele-sales. He's probably one of the best simply because he understands the side of his customer or prospect.

Here's what he has to say. Jason points out that in any sales environment, there is an emphasis on production...

how much is sold. A business without sales is not in business for long, so there is sometimes a grotesque emphasis on sales results. Nothing particularly new there to most of us. Fundamentally, that would seem to be okay. But on a tactical, everyday level, we bombard sales reps with techniques, contests and incentives designed specifically to maximize the dollar value of a sale.

Good sales people, say Jason, are hungry for these opportunities, "Add a little of this, a little of that, a touch more here and a tad more there...and et voila." A rep can double or triple the value of the sale, increase commissions and impress the heck out of the boss. Like the good side of the Force, if the approach and offer are value added and professionally implemented, everyone wins.

Enter the dark side. The trouble is that some of the techniques suggested in this book can be, and sometimes are, abused. At some point, the customer or the prospect grows weary of the mindless and valueless techniques.

At some point, they tend to resent the efforts as being anywhere from mildly annoying to blatantly dishonest.

The Cost of Abuse and Misuse
Maybe the cost of abusing or misusing add-on selling is obvious. Nonetheless, I think it is vital that we take a good, long, hard look at the issue so that you don't get tempted by the dark side.

Lost Customers
Misused add-on selling tactics can lose customers. What more can be said? If your rep is too aggressive, if the add-on product is of poor quality, if the delivery of the message is poor, etc., you're going to annoy the customer. Left unchecked, you'll lose them for good. You can calculate the cost by determining the "lifetime value of the customer." Balance this against the cost of acquiring the customer

and you have a compelling financial case to avoid abuse of add-on selling.

Negative Word of Mouth

There is another fallout if the add-on selling program is not implemented professionally. It's called negative word of mouth. Customers who have a poor experience with a company that abuses add on selling tells other customers AND potential customers. We touched on this when discussing complaints. People who have a bad experience with your company tend to tell 11 others. Bottom line? Customers simply stop buying. They never tell you why. They just don't come back.

Lost Sales

So, it goes without saying that lost customers and lost products means lost sales, lost revenues, reduced cash flow.

Internal Backlash –Turnover and Recruiting

Here's something else. If an add-on program is improperly implemented, the rep also suffers. Customers and prospects tend to have a nasty streak if they feel the service is manipulative or aggressive. I don't know if you noticed, but sometimes they can be downright rude. They lecture the rep. They'll harangue. They'll swear. They'll hang up or walk away. This is frustrating and discouraging for the average rep. It leads to burnout.

When reps get burned out, they turn ugly or they leave. If they turn ugly, their negative attitude is cast upon the customer, who in turn, dishes it back. Everyone loses.

Another implication is this: word gets out that your call center or work place is unprofessional at best or unethical, at worst. Attracting good quality workers becomes tougher because no one want to work in that environment. You can apply a cost to this as well. The cost of constant recruiting, selection, and training in terms of time and money, can be significant.

Is it worth it?

Nope. Nyet. Nadda.

So, don't be tempted

10 Ways to Avoid the Dark Side

1. Think Long Term
Don't expect immediate results.
Add-on selling looks simple enough and it is…if you take the time to do it right. This is vital to understand.

You need to start small. Experiment. Test the abilities of the reps. You need to gauge your customer's reactions. You must ensure that you can fulfill on every order. You must think about how you want to train and reward your reps. You must have job aids to help make the program success-ful. You must ensure that all other departments are on board and capable of handling the workload.

When you think long term, it means you have to sit down and plan it out. The process of planning will help you avoid the Dark Side pitfalls. If you plan it out and imple-ment it effectively, add-on selling will last a lifetime. Avoid the planning and implement it poorly, and add-on selling will be a disaster.

2. Don't Dump Junk
This is VERY IMPORTANT.

You'll be tempted. Believe me. From time to time, you'll be tempted to use add-on selling to help you get rid of in-ventory that no one wanted to buy in the first place. I am talking about lousy products. Products that don't work. Products that fall apart. Products about which you have had numerous complaints. You know the scenario: you bought a product that simply isn't turning because it stinks. It's costing you money sitting in inventory. This is when the dark side really rears its ugly head.

Resist it. If the product is of poor quality, write it off. Don't use it and risk losing your customers. It will haunt you. It will bite you in the backside.

3. Practice Full Disclosure
However, this doesn't mean you CAN'T sell items that are not moving. Hey, let's face it, not all products are a big hit. Some get outdated quickly, while others are limited in what they do, or they are unattractive (e.g., ugly colors), or they have a scratch or a dent. The product is fine, but there is something that has slowed down sales. You can and should attempt to sell these items as add-ons, provided that you are up-front and honest with your customer.

For example, Custom Checks in Winnipeg did this very thing a while ago. They had a product called the "counter check" which had become outdated and, in fact, they had written it off. The call center manager however, came up with an idea of how banks could use the product on a one-time basis. They scripted a message for the reps and when customers called, the rep explained the product was discontinued but suggested how a bank might use it. Of course, the price was ridiculously low. A real bargain. But it worked because their customers completely understood what was going on.

No one wants a surprise. If the slow-moving item is an Ugly, vomit-looking yellow, be sure to tell the client. If there is a scratch or a dent, tell them. If their software is a version or two below the current, speak up.

4. Guarantee the Add-On

You avoid the effects of the Dark Side if you guarantee all the items you sell. You can tell your customer this at any time. A guarantee brings peace of mind. It brings trust.

In the same breath, make your return policy easy and hassle-free. If buyer remorse kicks in after the customer has taken possession of the product, don't make it difficult for them to return it. Let them. This is easy stuff if you are thinking long-term. Thinking long-term anticipates the customer returning items.

5. Limit Your Add-on

This is a tip that can save you some grief. Limit the number of add-ons that you offer to one. Or at the very, very most, two. Remember, your customer called you for something other than the add-on sell. The add-on sell in on YOUR agenda, not theirs.

Respect that.

Not too long ago, I called Time-Life in response to a TV ad to order some CDs featuring music from the 70's. Remembering those hazy, crazy days of summer, I picked up the phone and placed the order. When I finished, the order rep mechanically launched into a cross-sell on another item. I found no value or need for the item and declined.

Then the rep continued with another. Nope, I said. And then, defying all odds, she hit me with a *third* add-on broadside. By now, I was annoyed. If she had attempted another cross-sell she would have lost the order. Customers have a tolerance level. Don't push it.

6. Relate

Try to relate your add-on sell with the original sale. It makes the selling process easier and more successful. Victoria's Secret does well because their cross-sell relates to clothing. Lee Valley Tools does well because their add-on sales relate to tools.

But, let me qualify this a bit. Purchasing an add-on product is sometimes an impulse buy on the part of the customer. Sometimes, you can appeal to that impulse buy. For instance, when I purchased a high-end roller ball pen from Levenger, the rep offered me a tiny bean bag frog. Ostensibly, the frog was a paperweight. In reality, it was an impulse buy.

My point here is, think about your items and try to relate them. Some won't relate and that's okay. The problem is that you can go overboard on selling unrelated items and this can irk your customers over time. You need only gauge the sale's success to fully assess this.

7. Survey Your Customers
Do you really want to know if you irk or please your customers with your add-on strategies?

If so, from time to time, survey them. Call a few dozen of your customers and ask them how they feel about the add-on. Try to gauge if their reaction is one of annoyance, indifference, or positive acceptance. If they are annoyed or indifferent, find out why. Determine if it was the add-on strategy itself, or the products, or the reps who delivered the message.

8. Avoid High Pressure
If you are reading this with a pen in hand, put a great big circle and a star right here so you never forget.

You or your reps are going to hear objections like these from time to time:

"I'd like to think about it..."

"Maybe next time..."

"No, I am not interested..."

"I'll have to call you back on that..."

When you hear these types of objections...

...leave them alone.

Don't challenge them.

Don't try to overcome them.

Don't use clever objections-handling techniques. Don't.

Right now, I'll bet many sales trainers and managers are having a minor coronary.

I don't care.

I have said this several times: The customer called you, NOT to buy your add-on, but to buy other products, to inquire about services, because of a complaint, or because of service related issues, etc. The add-on is YOUR agenda, not THEIRS. Do not make the add-on sale a major sale.

Why?

Because that's exactly what customers tell us they hate. They hate the high pressure of a rep haranguing them about buying something they don't want. In a way, your add-on is an off-the-cuff offer. You don't really know if the customer needs the item, so you are taking a chance. If the chance doesn't pay off immediately, fine. This applies to all add-on applications. If the customer doesn't want to give you market intelligence, don't push it. If they don't have a referral, don't press it. And so on. Thank the customer and move on.

Your add-on strategy is doomed if you use high pressure. Maybe not today, maybe not tomorrow but someday, and soon, it will catch up to you.

9. Train To Avoid the Pain
I call it the Kiss Of Death.

In 12 years of consulting and training, if there is one mistake I have seen repeated over and over and over, it is a lack of training. For whatever reason, many departments are reluctant to invest in formal training. Their program fails, or at best, gets marginal results and they wonder why.

Training builds confidence level of the reps. Pure and simple. And make no mistake about it, confidence sells. Yes, it takes time and effort and, sometimes, money. Get over it. Do it right or don't do it all.

Train your reps (or yourself) in two key areas. The first area is product knowledge. If you are going to offer products or services, make sure you know a little about the product. The items need to be described and customers will have questions.

Second, train your reps on the Four-Step Process. It should eventually come automatically, and when it does, sales will soar. Use this book or, heck, give me a call and I'll provide you with a training session. (How's that for a real blatant add-on pitch?)

Let me conclude by putting it in another way. If you don't formally train your reps and only rely on a few brief instructions, you are beating a path to the dark side. Sooner or later, one or more of your reps will stray. This will impact your customers at some point. Look at training as preventive medicine.

10. Monitor for Peace of Mind

I am constantly dumbfounded by the number of call centers that rarely, if ever, monitor calls. I am sure the managers are much too busy compiling reports, attending meetings and chatting to take the time and listen to what is being said. Pardon the sarcasm, but you'll never know if the Dark Side has visited your department unless you monitor calls.

Monitoring means listening to calls. It means listening on a regular and continuous basis, not once a month for 15 minutes. If you are a manager, you cannot possibly implement a successful add-on program without committing to the monitoring process.

Monitoring ensures that your reps are following the standards you created (and trained for) for the add-on process. It ensures that they are doing it and that they are doing it RIGHT. That's called quality. Monitoring helps you gauge your customer's reaction. That's called customer satisfaction. Monitoring helps you detect those who are flagrantly abusing the process. That's called fraud. (And trust me, it happens.)

11. Coach, Coach, and Coach Some More

I just read a survey where managers claim they give sufficient coaching, while their employees claim they get little or no coaching at all. Huh? What gives? There's a gap.

Here's the scoop. Training is great. It is vital. It is necessary. But if you train and you don't coach, the skills and techniques taught will diminish in a week. I call it the "Whittle Effect". Here's what happens. The moment after your reps leave the training session, they begin to whittle away what they learned. The first to go on the Four-Step Process will be the benefit. They'll lop that off in a day. A short while later, the bridge will be amputated. And finally, the close will simply evaporate into thin air. You'll be left with a vague offer. Everyone, and I mean everyone, loses.

I am not exaggerating. As a trainer, I know that reps cannot possibly retain all that they have learned in a workshop or a seminar without some help. They forget things. They apply things incorrectly. They don't see the logic in Something, so they dismiss it. This is human nature. We all go back to our comfort zones.

Left unchecked, within a week, and I mean this, they will be back to where they were before the training. Or worse, and here's where you need to worry, your reps will have created a Frankenstein version of an add-on selling technique that is sure to frighten, if not kill the client. Of course, that's where the Dark Side kicks in.

Coaching has to be a daily routine.

This is especially true with customer service reps, help desk employees, and others who typically don't sell because they weren't hired to sell. The add-on sale will be new, different and uncomfortable. You need to support your reps by coaching, otherwise, they'll get discouraged. They'll either quite attempting the add-on or they'll become a Frankenstein.

Okay. Got it, Coach?

12. Watch Your Reward System

I am all for giving your reps some sort of stipend, reward, bonus or commission for a successful add-on sale. After all, the rep is doing more for you and your company. He or she is generating more revenue, applying a higher skill level and taking on the risk of rejection. Recognition of some sort is important.

But incentives, if too large or too rewarding, can be the fast track to the Dark Side.

Let me tell you a true story. A while ago, I was working with a company that sold products to professionals. Without getting into detail, I discovered (through monitoring) that several of the reps were abusing the up-selling add-on. You see, the commission rewarded gross sales. The higher the gross, the higher the commission.

What happened however, is that these reps would add an up-sell order to the original order *even though the customer had declined.* I confronted one of the reps about this when a customer called to complain about being overshipped and overcharged. The rep pointed out, rather pleased with herself, that half the clients don't even catch the error. Those that do, call immediately and the reps respond with apologies and credits or returns. Ultimately, she justified the approach by convincing herself that the customer would "use the product anyway".

What a clever, if not insidious little approach to selling. That worked for a while until this happened to the same customers several times. The gig was up. The reps and several others were terminated, but not before the damage was done. This might have been nipped in the bud if monitoring had been conducted on a regular basis but, quite frankly, the monetary reward was so great, that it was a natural temptation.

Lesson learned.

13. Strike Fast and Hard
One hates to have to think this way but burying our heads in the sand won't change behavior. The last tip to avoid the Dark Side is, if you see abuse, strike hard and strike fast.

The above company investigated and discovered that the abuse was rampant and affected numerous clients. The termination was fast and furious. Bravo. Excise the tumor. Stamp it out. But in my opinion, they omitted one thing. They did not use the situation to educate and communicate with their reps. It was rather hush, hush. The message of fraud (what else can you call it) was left to the internal grapevine.

Broadcast it. Let everyone know the consequences.

Summary
Let me say it again and summarize quickly. Don't kill the goose that lays the golden egg.

Chapter 20

Summary of Add-On Selling

This is a really short chapter and its objective is to pull a few things together.

Here's a fact. Add-On Selling is a powerful selling technique that can be used to generate more sales or more sales opportunities. As I write this, the economy is sluggish at best. The markets are taking a beating. Customers and prospects are hesitant and leery about purchase decisions. Getting a hold of them is even tougher.

What this means to you is that you have to make the most of every opportunity from every call you make or take. You simply don't have the chances you once did. It's tough to sell at the best of times. You must professionally and respectfully seize the moment and squeeze every ounce of potential from every single contact.

Add-on selling is easy to implement. It consists of four simple steps. That's it. Four simple, yet highly effective steps. Add them on to the end of your calls or visits. As my teenage sons often say, "It's a no brainer!"

Remember two things:

First, customers and prospects tell us (you) that they don't buy more from us (you) and that there are two reasons why they don't buy more from us (you):

1. We don't educate them on our offers, products and services, and

2. we don't ask them to take action

Second, customers and prospects tell us (you) that they do not mind add-on selling techniques when professionally and respectfully presented. In fact, they want to be educated. They want to know about offers and specials. They don't mind being asked for referrals, or whatever, if they have received exceptional service. They like to reciprocate. I am not telling you this. *They* are telling you this. Listen to *them*.

Ultimately, it's your *choice* .

You have a choice to continue selling and servicing in your current manner or not. You have a choice to implement add-on selling or not. It's up to you.

If you don't implement add-on selling, *nothing will change*.

Your sales results will remain the same .

And heck, you might even make a pretty good living providing basic selling and servicing skills. But, the difference between pretty good and great can be measured in very small doses. Ask any professional athlete. Ask Tiger Woods. Better yet, ask all those who compete against Tiger.

Great sales reps do a lot of little things superbly well. Add-on selling is a highly consultative approach to consulting with your customers. It makes them happy and it makes you more effective and successful. And, sometimes, more wealthy.

Just a few more points.

Answer these three questions:

> 1. What's stopping you from implementing add-on selling?
>
> 2. What's the worst that can happen if you do?
>
> 3. What's the best that can happen?

Give add-on selling a good ,honest try and you will move from the realm of mediocre to the realm of great.

And let me know how it goes.

Call me or e-mail. Tell me your success. Tell me of your failures. Ask for advice. I'll be glad to help.

And at the risk of beating a horse to death, remember, it's your choice.

Jim Domanski
613 591 1998
jdomanski@igs.net
www.teleconceptsconsulting.com

Get Jim's Other Book:
"Profiting By Phone"
248 pages, paperback

Regardless of whether you're a seasoned
veteran or rookie rep, you'll find ideas you'll use
right away. Here's just a small sample of the
hundreds of ideas you'll get in this book:

• how to write call guides and scripts that get
  results
• how to quickly qualify—and disqualify—prospects
• words to avoid that are sure to kill the sale
• how to build long-term relationships with your customers
• mistakes to avoid when handling objections, and what to say instead
• word-for-word voice mail tactics that help avoid "voice mail jail"
• strategies for overcoming fear on the phone, and of the phone

Plus Much More!

> *"I was so inspired by your book, I made a list of goals,*
> *including how to get my dream house. I'm halfway*
> *through the list after only 2 weeks! We're offering the*
> *material in your book as a six-week seminar to our tele-*
> *marketing/telesales reps, and ordered 25 more copies."*
> Carollyn Farrar, Inside Sales Manager, CFI ProServices,

84 Chapters and Hundreds of Ideas You'll Use Right Now!
Written in Jim's highly entertaining style and format, this book is
fun to read and easy to use. Whether you are an inside or outside
sales rep, supervisor or manager, this practical and informative
book will help you generate more revenue and income, increase
the volume and quality of your leads, and help reduce rejection
and burnout. Order today!

$29.00 (U.S. Shipping $3.50, Canadian shipping $7.00)

Call 800-326-7721, or go to
http://www.BusinessByPhone.com/PBP.htm

To Get More Copies of This Book

To get additional copies of this book, photocopy or remove this form, or call or fax us with the necessary information. *(Inquire about quantity discounts. Also, bookstore and dealer inquiries welcome.)*

Yes, please send me _____ copies of "Add-On Selling," at $29 (U.S. funds) each (+$4 shipping in the U.S., $7 Canada, overseas charged at cost.)

Name_____

Company_____

Address_____

City_____State_____Zip _____

Phone_____

Fax_____

e-mail_____

❏ Visa/MC/AMEX/Discover

#_____

sig._____exp._____

❏ Check /Money Order Enclosed *(U.S. Funds Only)*

- **Phone** your order to **1-800-326-7721** , or (402)895-9399.

- **Fax** your order to (402)896-3353.

- Mail **your order to Business By Phone, 13254-B1 Stevens St., Omaha, NE, 68137.**

- Online at www.BusinessByPhone.com/PBP.htm